WORD WIZARD

Literacy Skills and Activities

Alison Ginnell

g GILL EDUCATION

Contents

How to Use this Book

Comprehension strategies

This book continues building on the comprehension strategies learned at earlier levels of the *Word Wizard* series. Pupils are now exposed to a variety of engaging activities designed to foster their comprehension skills before, during and after reading.

 This symbol indicates a comprehension activity to be carried out **before reading**.

 This symbol indicates a comprehension activity to be carried out **during reading**.

 This symbol indicates a comprehension activity to be carried out **after reading**.

Care has been taken to make these activities as general as possible so that they may be applied to other texts such as a class novel.

Some activities are repeated in order to give pupils sufficient practice in important strategies that will help them to use these strategies independently with future texts.

For a detailed explanation of all comprehension strategies, see page vi.

Vocabulary development

 Use your dictionary to find out the meaning of the **bold** words below.

A stop sign appears before each comprehension reading passage, asking pupils to use their dictionary to find out the meaning of the bold words in the text before reading. This is designed to facilitate the teaching of tricky vocabulary prior to reading the text.

Cloze procedure

A cloze procedure closely linked to the reading passage has been included in each unit. In the first four units (leading up to October mid-term), the missing words are provided in a word box. In subsequent units, the answers can be found on pages 113–114. This allows for much needed practice, helps with confidence-building and develops familiarity with cloze procedures.

Dictation

Three dictation sentences are provided for each unit, incorporating the phonics and grammar taught. Suggestions are provided for extension activities or further revision of grammar.

Assessment

A self-assessment feature appears below each dictation activity.

Two units dedicated to revision and assessment are provided at the end of the second and third terms. Each includes a special four-day section designed to prompt meaningful revision of phonics and grammar before assessment begins.

Extra

Each unit concludes with a suggested activity for extension work that facilitates integration within the areas of art, debate, drama and others.

Genre writing approach

The series takes a unique approach to genre writing. At this level, genre writing follows a four-week approach, with a fortnight spent on each unit. Two units are dedicated to each genre.

Discrete oral language activities act as building blocks for genre writing.

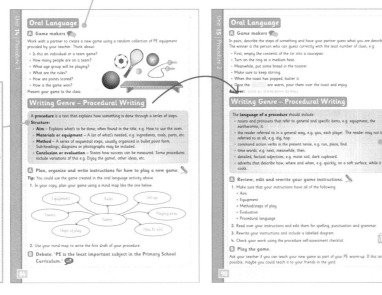

The first unit dedicated to each genre explores the **structure** of the genre. Pupils are asked to **plan and draft** a piece of writing, usually linked to the comprehension topic.

The second unit dedicated to each genre introduces the **language and grammar** that pupils are expected to include in the genre. They are then asked to **edit and rewrite** the piece of writing drafted in the previous unit.

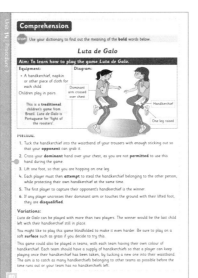

The reading passage serves as a template for the genre. The teacher can refer to this while outlining the structure of the genre, simply through discussion, or by having pupils highlight or underline the various elements.

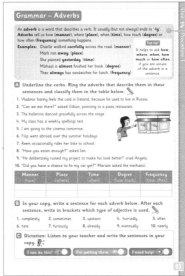

Grammar activities are linked to the genre wherever appropriate.

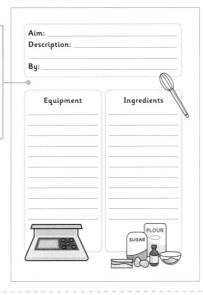

An editable writing frame is provided online to allow pupils to publish their work for an audience.

A self-assessment checklist is also provided to help pupils edit and self-assess their work.

Comprehension Strategies Guide

Predicting (P) means guessing what will happen. By looking at what has happened in the story already, you can make informed predictions about what might happen next. A book's cover, title, blurb, chapter titles and images also provide clues to help you.

Making Connections (MC) means linking information in the text to something in your own life (text to self), something that you read somewhere else (text to text) or something that you heard about on the television or the radio or from another person (text to world).

Visualising (V) means creating mental pictures based on the text and images.

Questioning (Q): I wonder… This involves asking questions about what you are reading while you read. Keep your mind active and dig deeper into the text.

Word Attack (WA): When you get stuck on a word, use the following bank of Word Attack skills to help you figure it out:

'weather' we, wet, the, her, he, eat, tea, heat	Look for a smaller word in the word.	al-li-ga-tor	Sound out the word. Break it up. Chunk it.
l a ke b oa t d r ea m	Look at the beginning, middle and end of the word.	Prefix Root Suffix	Do you recognise any prefixes, suffixes or root words?
	Look at the images. Is there a clue?	**SKIP IT!**	Skip the word and read the sentence to the end.
	Make a guess. What would make sense?	Context	Use the words around it. Put it in context.
	Go back and re-read.		Use your background knowledge.
DICTIONARY	Use your dictionary or thesaurus.		Picture the word in your mind. What do you see?

Determining Importance (DI) means deciding what is relevant or irrelevant. If you were to tell a stranger what the text was about, what would be the key points?

Inferring (I) means reading between the lines.

Clarifying (C) means figuring out a word, a phrase or an idea that you don't understand. Don't give up! Re-read the text or ask for help to understand it more clearly.

Summarising (S) means choosing the key points from the text.

Synthesising (Sy) means using all of your comprehension strategies to understand what you are reading.

Skimming is a **skill** that involves having a quick look through the text to get a general understanding. Headings, images and words that are **bold**, *italicised* or underlined can be useful clues.

Scanning is a **skill** that involves reading quickly through the text to find specific or important information.

Man on the Moon

Comprehension Strategies

Top tip!

Look over the Comprehension Strategies Guide on page vi to revise each strategy.

A Before reading: I wonder …

Use the strategy of **Questioning**. Fill in the thought bubbles with questions about the text.

I wonder

I wonder

I wonder

B During reading: Fabulous five

Use the strategy of **Determining Importance**. While reading, record five key words in the text. Then, in groups, compare your 'fabulous five' and justify why you thought these were the most important words in the text.

C After reading: Oral summary

Use the strategy of **Summarising**. In pairs, summarise the main points of the text. Present your summary orally to the class.

D After reading: If I was …

Use the strategy of **Making Connections**. Use the main points of the text that you and your partner listed above. Take on the character of one of the men in the text. Think about how you would have felt and thought and why you acted the way you did at each point.

Comprehension

 STOP! Use your dictionary to find out the meaning of the **bold** words below.

✤ THE AMERICAN STAR ✤

MAN ON THE MOON

BOB LEE   THUR. JULY 24TH 1969

TODAY, THURSDAY JULY 24th, Americans celebrate the return of the *Apollo 11* astronauts.

Last week, on July 16th, the **colossal** *Saturn V* rocket lifted off from NASA's Kennedy Space Centre in Merritt Island, Florida. Aboard were heroic astronauts Neil A. Armstrong, Edwin 'Buzz' Aldrin and Michael Collins. This comes just eight years after the **Soviets** sent the first man into space; an event which caused President Kennedy's challenge to put a man on the moon before the end of the decade.

Buzz Aldrin on the moon

The **trio** travelled a quarter of a million miles to reach the **coveted** destination. They arrived in lunar **orbit** on July 19th. Once the crew had reached orbit, Armstrong and Aldrin entered the Lunar Module of the spacecraft, nicknamed 'Eagle', which would transport them to the moon's surface. Collins remained in orbit overhead, manning the **Command Module** 'Columbia' that would eventually take them home.

As hundreds of millions across the globe watched in **awe**, the Lunar Module undocked and safely touched down at the Sea of Tranquillity on the moon's surface on July 20th. Upon landing, Armstrong's voice crackled from the speakers at NASA's Mission Control in Houston. Simply stating, "The Eagle has landed," Armstrong **uttered** the first words ever spoken on the moon.

Six hours later, Armstrong climbed down the ladder of the Eagle and became the first man to walk on the moon. Once there, Armstrong **proclaimed** the words that are sure to be recorded in

From left to right: Armstrong, Collins, Aldrin

history books for years to come: "That's one small step for a man, one giant leap for mankind." Moments later, Aldrin became the second man on the moon.

The men spent a total of two and a half hours exploring the lunar surface. While there, the pair **deployed** the first human experiments carried out outside of this planet. They also collected about twenty-two kilograms of **priceless** moon rocks for study on their return to Earth.

In addition to these experiments, Armstrong and Aldrin **unveiled** a **plaque** on the part of the Lunar Module that was to be **discarded** on the moon's surface. "Here men from the planet Earth first set foot upon the moon. July 1969 AD. We came in peace for all mankind," it announced. The American flag was also planted and left there as a reminder of the greatest scientific **accomplishment** by mankind to date.

The pair then returned to the upper part of the Lunar Module and **jettisoned** off the moon's surface to rejoin Collins in the Command Module and begin their journey home. The Columbia returned to Earth today, landing in the Pacific Ocean, having completed its **remarkable** mission. The explorers were **retrieved** by a helicopter. They, along with their **precious** lunar samples, have been placed in **quarantine** until their health and safety can be **confirmed**.

Meanwhile, the world waits in **anticipation** to welcome our heroes home.

A In your copy, go investigate.

1. From where did the *Apollo 11* mission launch?

2. Who was the first man to walk on the moon?

3. Where is the Sea of Tranquillity?

4. Why didn't Michael Collins walk on the moon?

5. What did Armstrong and Aldrin do while they were on the moon?

6. When did the astronauts return to Earth?

B In your copy, give your opinion.

1. Why do you think Armstrong said, "That's one small step for a man, one giant leap for mankind"?

2. How do you think you would have felt if you were Michael Collins?

3. Why do you think the astronauts were kept in quarantine when they returned?

4. Why do you think the Sea of Tranquillity is so named?

5. The competition between Russia and America to be first to explore space was called the 'Space Race'. Who do you think won the race? Why?

6. Write the message that you would have left on the moon if you had been first person there.

C Vocabulary

Search the text for synonyms (words that have the same meaning) of 'said'. Write them below and add to the list with the help of a thesaurus.

D Cloze procedure: 'The First Man in Space'. Fill in the blanks.

minutes pilot blasted Space return first Americans manmade historical of

With the launch _____ Sputnik 1 in 1957, Russia was the first to send a _____ satellite into orbit. Eager to continue their success and beat the _____ in the '_____ Race', Yuri Gagarin, a Soviet fighter _____, was chosen as the _____ cosmonaut to be sent into space. On April 12th 1961, the *Vostok 1* spacecraft _____ off from the Soviet launch site. Yuri spent 108 _____ in orbit, travelling around the Earth once. On his _____, he was hailed as an international hero, travelling around the world to celebrate the _____ Soviet achievement.

Yuri Gagarin

Phonics – Silent Letters

Silent letters are letters that we do not pronounce when reading or saying words. They are important for spelling and to help us tell the difference between some words, e.g. night and **k**night.

A Cross out the incorrect words. Highlight the silent letters. Look up any words you don't know in your dictionary.

1. "I am starving! It's been **hours** / **ours** since the last time I **eight** / **ate**!" cried **Sam** / **psalm**.

2. Victor's **aunt** / **ant** taught him how to **nit** / **knit**.

3. The queen ended her fifty-year **rain** / **reign** by giving her **air** / **heir** the throne.

4. The **gnu** / **knew** is my favourite animal to see at the zoo.

5. Sania was forced to **ring** / **wring** out her clothes after she was caught in the **rain** / **reign**.

6. "You **need** / **knead** to **need** / **knead** the dough before rolling it out," explained Hania.

7. My birthday cake was so delicious I ate the **whole** / **hole** thing by myself.

8. Mum thinks I lost my **new** / **knew** shoes, but I **know** / **no** they're under my bed.

B Underline the silent letters in the words below. Make lists of the words with the same silent letters.

thumb	salmon	debt	wrote	solemn	pneumonia
sword	autumn	plumber	calm	psychiatrist	design
folks	climb	wrestler	column	gnome	raspberry
doubt	answer	foreign	chalk	receipt	government
wreathe	resign	cupboard	colonel	condemn	campaign

Silent	Silent	Silent	Silent	Silent	Silent

C In your copy, write a sentence using one word from each list above.

Grammar – Capital Letters

We use a capital letter for:

- the start of a sentence.
- the pronoun 'I'.
- the names of people, as well as their titles, e.g. Dr Watson, Mrs Doubtfire.
- the names of places and monuments.
- the main words in the titles of books, films, TV programmes, etc.
- the days of the week, months and festivals (but not the seasons).
- languages, nationalities and religions.

A Ring the words that should have a capital letter.

1. when i was in new york during the summer, i saw the statue of liberty.

2. mr jones takes the bus from cavan to donegal every friday.

3. i speak english and irish, and my friend dominika speaks polish and russian.

4. muslims follow islam. they celebrate eid ul adha and read the qur'an.

5. 'dr zonko's science lab' is my favourite television programme. it starts in may.

Remember to use the correct punctuation.

- A **full stop** (.) marks the end of a sentence.
- A **question mark** (?) is used at the end of a question.
- An **exclamation mark** (!) is used for interjections like "Help!" or "Phew!", or to put emphasis on a sentence.
- A **comma** (,) separates words in a list or spoken language from the rest of a sentence.
- **Speech marks** (" ") are placed at the start of a spoken sentence and after the full stop, comma, question mark or exclamation mark to show direct speech.

B In your copy, rewrite this passage using the correct punctuation marks (38) and capital letters (41).

it was saturday and jacob alex mum and dad were on their way to dublin what should we do when we get there asked dad i want to go shopping said mum me too cried alex would you like to do some sight-seeing jacob asked dad yes cried jacob when they got to dublin mum and alex went to grafton street to do some shopping meanwhile jacob and dad went for a walk and saw the spire trinity college and the gpo on the way home jacob read *charlie and the chocolate factory* which mum had bought him that was the best day ever exclaimed alex

C Dictation: Listen to your teacher and write the sentences in your copy.

I can do this! 　　I'm getting there. 　　I need help!

5

Oral Language

A Sound bite

In pairs, research and write a recount on a news event happening in school or the world at the moment. Organise your recount into a thirty-second report. Try to include reported speech in your sound bite, e.g. 'Local police are reported to have said they are working hard on the case.' 'The principal exclaimed, "What a wonderful show!" when the concert was over.'

Writing Genre – Recount Writing

Daily News

The purpose of a **recount** is to retell or recount past experiences or events. Recounts may be personal, factual or imaginative.

Structure:

- **Setting** – Set the scene by including who, where, when, what, why and how.
- **Events** – Told in time order; begin a new paragraph for each new event when changing subject, place, time or event.
- **Concluding statement** – Can be in the form of the author's feelings in a personal recount or an evaluative comment in a factual recount.

A Plan, organise and write an imaginative newspaper article in the form of a recount.

Choose one of the following headlines:

- 'Local schoolchild saves the day'
- 'Disaster at the MTV Video Music Awards!'
- 'Mystery of disappeared sporting hero is finally solved'

1. In your copy, plan your recount using a plan like the one below.

Newspaper article: _____

Setting

Who	Where	When	What	Why	How

Events

Event 1	Event 2	Event 3	Event 4	Event 5

Concluding statement

2. Use the information in your plan to write the first draft of your recount.

B Debate: 'The moon landing was faked.'

Letter from a World War I Soldier

Comprehension Strategies

A Before reading: Crystal ball

Use the strategy of **Predicting**. Look at the title and image and use your crystal ball to predict what will happen in the text.

> I predict that…
>
> I imagine that…
>
> I think that…
>
> I think that… will happen, because…
>
> I wonder if…
>
> Maybe… will happen, because…

Return to the crystal ball after reading and predict what will happen next.

B During reading: Five senses

Use the strategy of **Visualising**. Stop reading and record what you can see, hear, smell, taste and touch.

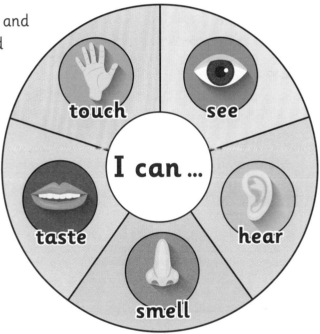

I can …

touch · see · hear · smell · taste

C After reading: Interview

Use the strategy of **Inferring**. In your copy, make a list of interview questions that you would ask the main character in the text. In pairs, answer each other's questions using evidence from the text.

D During reading: Plot review

Use the strategy of **Synthesising**. As a class, list the main events of the text on flash cards. Next, hold the cards and line up in the order that each event happened. Then, rate the event you are holding. Hold it up high if it was very exciting, hold it at your chest if it was normal and hold it low if it was not very exciting at all. Discuss and compare your reviews. This could be repeated with various different reactions to the text, e.g. sad, happy, interesting, etc.

Top tip!

'Synthesising' means using all of your comprehension strategies to understand what you are reading.

Comprehension

STOP! Use your dictionary to find out the meaning of the **bold** words below.

Letter from a World War I Soldier

Cornwall,
England

France,
October 1917

Dearest Mother and Father,

I am writing to you this morning from my miserable **bunker** somewhere in France – none of us are sure exactly where. As I write, aeroplanes **soar** overhead, **eager** to cause **havoc** in enemy **trenches**, so I must be quick. How are you all at home? I hope Teresa and Jim are pulling their weight around the farm with me gone. Pass on my dearest love to them. I miss them both terribly.

Firstly, I must thank you for your kind gift. I was delighted to receive your package before leaving for the front lines last month. It was very much **appreciated**. Spare socks, warm woollen hats and gloves are **essential** for keeping well in this **harsh** weather. I will think of you **fondly** while I wear them, Mother.

Conditions here are **horrendous**. Not long after we arrived, our trench flooded. Now we are all terrified of developing trench foot, a condition almost as much of a death sentence as an order over the top. **Meanwhile**, our food is regularly **infested** with rats. We eat it anyway, as there is no way to know when more **rations** will be provided.

Last week, we were sent over the top. It was **horrific**. I felt foolish **brandishing** my **bayonet** against heavy **artillery** fire; like a small child **confronting** a much bigger, stronger bully. We set out with thirty in our **platoon** and returned with only twelve. The following day, we noticed that some of the men who were injured during the fighting had developed infections caused by the damp here. **Subsequently**, my commanding officer had them **transferred** to a hospital back at base camp for fear they might **succumb** to their infections.

Following our battle tonight, I hope to move back to the support lines in order to get a break after these **gruelling** past weeks. Our commanding officer has said that another **battalion** are on their way to **relieve** us. I cannot tell you how grateful I will be for this much needed rest. I dearly miss you all and eagerly await your next letter.

I remain your ever loving son,
Edward Walker

Soldiers in the trenches

A **In your copy, go investigate.**

1. From where is Edward writing this letter?

2. How might the aeroplanes overhead 'cause havoc in enemy trenches'?

3. What did Edward's parents send him?

4. When did Edward and his platoon arrive at the front lines?

5. Describe the conditions in the trenches.

6. Why did the commanding officer send the men back to base camp?

B **In your copy, give your opinion.**

1. What do you think the weather is like where Edward is? Explain.

2. Who do you think Teresa and Jim are?

3. Would you have eaten the food knowing that it was infested with rats? Why/Why not?

4. What do you think 'over the top' means?

5. Why do you think Edward specifically thanks his mother for the gifts?

6. How do you think Edward is feeling while writing this letter?

C **Vocabulary**

1. Read back over the text and underline the words that link events together in time, e.g. then, next. Write a list below. Add your own linking time words to the list.

2. In your copy, choose some of the words above to write in sentences. Pick a number to challenge yourself.

D **Cloze procedure: 'World War I Trenches'. Fill in the blanks.**

belong   rats   conditions   using   defence   about   trenches   cross   no   in   during

World War I was known for _____ trench warfare. Trenches were long, narrow ditches dug into the ground as a _____ against the enemy. Lines and lines of _____ were dug by both the Allies and the Central Powers. Between the trenches was a stretch of land called '____ man's land'. This area did not _____ to either army. Soldiers had to _____ this stretch of land ____ order to attack the opposition. The soldiers spent much of their time down in the trenches, where _____ were horrendous. Many trenches were infested with _____, lice and nits and were muddy and smelly. It is estimated that _____ 2,490 km of trenches were dug _____ World War I.

9

Phonics – '-nge'

The '**g**' in '**-nge**' makes a /j/ sound, e.g. cha**nge**.

A Tick the correct '-nge' word to match each picture. Use your dictionary to help you if necessary.

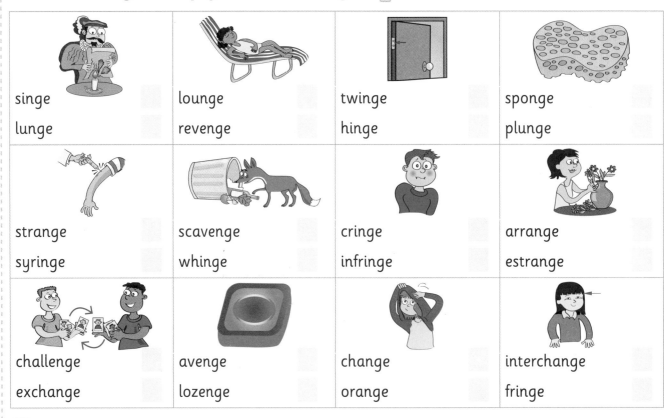

singe	lounge	twinge	sponge
lunge	revenge	hinge	plunge
strange	scavenge	cringe	arrange
syringe	whinge	infringe	estrange
challenge	avenge	change	interchange
exchange	lozenge	orange	fringe

B Complete the crossword using some of the '-nge' words not used above.

Down

1. To moan or complain
2. Odd or unusual
3. To dive quickly into water
4. A juicy, segmented fruit
5. Money returned when too much payment has been given

Across

6. Action taken in return for injury or offense
7. A difficult task
8. A sharp stab of pain

Unscramble the highlighted letters to answer this riddle:

What gets wetter the more it dries?

A _____

C In your copy, write a story at least six lines long. Use as many of the '-nge' words above as you can.

Grammar – Nouns

Nouns are naming words. They refer to people, places, things or animals.
Concrete nouns are nouns that you can see and touch, e.g. pineapple, wall.
Abstract nouns refer to feelings, qualities or ideas that cannot be seen or touched, e.g. hunger, joy.

A Underline the concrete nouns and ring the abstract nouns.

1. "We all have hope that the team will do well this year," sighed Ms Lynch.

2. Amin showed me great kindness when he let me share his lunch.

3. The villagers were stunned by the princess's beauty.

4. "Can you feel the warmth of the fire?" asked Callum.

5. Honesty, patience and good manners are very important qualities to my mum.

B Complete these by inserting the correct abstract nouns.

integrity   fear   elegance   sadness   confidence   honour

1. It is important not to show _____ when confronted with a wild animal.

2. Zoe was filled with _____ when her dog ran away.

3. "It is an _____ to witness such _____," exclaimed the presenter of the dance show.

4. William showed _____ when he did not let his friend copy his work.

5. The compliments I received about my art filled me with _____ .

Collective nouns are the names of groups of people, animals or things, e.g. a **coven** of witches, a **litter** of puppies, a **bunch** of flowers.

C Match each collective noun to the correct noun.

pride   herd   school   batch   pack   swarm   band   flock   parliament

1. A _____ of cattle   2. A _____ of cookies   3. A _____ of fish

4. A _____ of musicians   5. A _____ of owls   6. A _____ of lions

7. A _____ of flies   8. A _____ of birds   9. A _____ of wolves

D Dictation: Listen to your teacher and write the sentences in your copy.

I can do this!   I'm getting there.   I need help!

11

Oral Language

A Different recounts

A recount gives us an account of an event. Sometimes different recounts of the same event can give us different points of view or opinions. Read the newspaper report written during World War I and compare it to the letter from Edward. Discuss with your partner:

- Who might have written this?
- Who was the intended audience?
- Who or what might be influencing the author of this newspaper report?
- Why might the two recounts be different?

THE EVENING STAR

Success and High Morale at the Front Lines!

On Wednesday evening last, a brave platoon of mostly British soldiers charged the German lines.

Soldiers at the front have reported the mission a great success. "With minimal casualties for the allies and maximum devastation to the enemy, our boys at the front are making excellent progress," confirms Officer James Hall of the 5th Platoon, B Company.

The troops are said to be in high spirits following the latest round of victories.

Writing Genre – Recount Writing

The **language of a recount** should include:

- first or third person, e.g. I, we, he, they.
- simple past tense, e.g. sprinted, commanded, went, witnessed.
- mostly action verbs, e.g. saved, argued, discovered.
- linking time words, e.g. initially, eventually, after that, meanwhile.
- words and phrases to show time and place, e.g. beside the river, last weekend.
- reported speech, e.g. The boy's father reported that he was safe and well.

A Review, edit and rewrite your newspaper recount.

1. Make sure that your recount has all of the following:
   - Setting
   - A concluding statement
   - Recount language
   - Five sequential events
   - A 'photograph' of the event

2. Read over your recount and edit it for spelling, punctuation and grammar.

3. Rewrite your recount and try to:
   - consider the audience you are writing for and the point of view of the reporter.
   - entertain and inform your reader.

4. Check your work using the recount self-assessment checklist.

B Drama

Recounts can change depending on the author or audience. Consider how your newspaper article might change if it was intended for a news broadcast. Perform it for the class.

Green Team Elections

Comprehension Strategies

A Before reading: Dictionary chart

Use the strategy of **Word Attack** and the skill of **Scanning**. Scan the text and write any interesting words in the chart below. Look for clues in the text to try to figure out the meaning. Finally, use a dictionary to find out if you were right.

Word	Meaning from the text	Was I right?

B During reading: I think that … because …

Use the strategy of **Inferring**. As you read, stop along the way to make inferences with evidence from the text.

- Reading between the lines, I think that … because …
- I think this person is … because …
- I think this person will … because …
- I think … will happen because …
- The author wants me to think …

The author wants me to think …

C After reading: Crystal ball

Use the strategy of **Predicting**. Use your crystal ball to predict three things that will happen next. In pairs, compare your predictions. If any of your predictions are different, you must justify your ideas to your partner. Decide on three and share them with the class.

I predict that …

I imagine that …

I wonder if …

I think that …

I think that… will happen, because…

Maybe… will happen, because…

D After reading: Hot-seating

Use the strategies of **Questioning** and **Inferring**. In groups, compile a list of questions that you would like to ask each candidate. Hot-seat two children (in your group or as a class), who will answer these questions in character as Usman and Jane.

Comprehension

 STOP! Use your dictionary to find out the meaning of the **bold** words below.

Green Team Elections

Teachers, classmates and Principal, thank you for coming today. We are here to decide who will be the Green Team student leader in our school for the rest of the year. I am **honoured** to be in the position to speak before you today and to ask for your votes.

I would like to be the Green Team leader, as I have a huge interest in the environment and believe we have a responsibility to keep the world we live in clean and healthy. Some people might say that we are just children or that we are just one school, but I know that you agree with me when I say that everyone has their part to play in saving the environment.

I would be an excellent Green Team leader, because I am very **dedicated** and I work hard. In addition to this, I am really interested in saving the environment and I have loads of ideas for what the Green Team can do this year to help get our school's first Green Flag, Litter and Waste.

If elected Green Team leader this year, I would like to run a number of **initiatives** and events that will help us to get our flag. Firstly, I think we should all take home our lunch rubbish to recycle. This will mean that there is very little waste in the school. Also, I would like to work with the teachers to organise weekend 'litter pick' days to help keep our school and the **surrounding** area clean and tidy.

Ladies and gentlemen, thank you for listening. I hope I have proved to you today that I have many interesting and **effective** ideas to bring to the Green Team and that I will make a good student leader. You should vote for me, because I am **passionate** about the environment and very hardworking. Thank you and remember, vote for Usman.

Usman

Hi everyone, thanks for coming. I'm here to tell you why you should vote for me to be the student leader of the Green Team this year.

I would like to be the Green Team student leader, because I think it will be a lot of fun. I am looking forward to organising a lot of meetings during the day and some trips for the Green Team also.

I think I should be the Green Team student leader, because I am good at speaking in front of people and I don't mind telling other people what to do. This is an important skill for the Green Team leader, because there will be lots of other students on the team and I will have to give them jobs.

Jane

If I am elected Green Team leader, I will get the school to give us our lunches. This means that we won't be bringing any rubbish into the school. Also, I will ban everyone from driving to school, because cars are harmful to the environment.

You should vote for me to be Green Team leader, because I am a lot of fun and I will make sure the teachers listen to all of our ideas. Also, if I am **elected**, I will throw a big party for the class. Thank you for listening. Vote Jane!

A In your copy, go investigate.

1. For which job do these students want to be elected?

2. Does their school have any Green Flags yet? How do you know?

3. Why does Usman want to be the Green Team leader?

4. What does Jane promise to do if she is elected?

5. How is the Green Team leader going to be decided?

6. How do you know that Usman is interested in the environment?

B In your copy, give your opinion.

1. Who would you vote for? Why?

2. Does Jane have good reasons for wanting to be the Green Team leader? Why/Why not?

3. Would you attend Usman's 'litter pick' days? Why/Why not?

4. Are all of Jane's ideas suitable and realistic? Explain.

5. Do you think that being the Green Team leader is an important job? Explain.

6. What would you do if you were the Green Team leader in your school?

C Tick 'fact' or 'opinion' for each statement.

	Fact	Opinion
1. Jane would make the best Green Team leader.		
2. It is important to care for the environment.		
3. Being on the Green Team is a lot of fun.		
4. The first Green Flag theme is Litter and Waste.		
5. Banning everyone from driving to school is a good idea.		

D Cloze procedure: 'Green Schools'. Fill in the blanks.

together write Citizenship Flag evaluate focus seven involve two environmental

The Green-Schools initiative is an _____ education programme and award scheme that encourages schools to actively care for the environment. Schools work _____ as a community, including teachers, students and parents. There are seven environmental themes for schools to _____ on: Litter and Waste, Energy, Water, Travel, Biodiversity and Global _____. Schools must complete the following _____ steps in order to complete an environmental theme: set up a Green-Schools committee, complete an environmental review, _____ an action plan, monitor and _____ the plan, carry out work in the classroom, inform and _____ the whole school community and write a green code. Once the school has completed each of these steps, which takes about _____ years, it is awarded a Green _____ for that theme.

Phonics – Homophones

> **Homophones** are words that sound the same, but are spelled differently and have different meanings, e.g. piece (a section of something) and peace (a time of quiet or non-war).

A Complete the crossword using a homophone for each clue.

Down

1. hole:
2. stationery:
3. serial:
4. deer:
5. week:
6. sealing:
10. altar:
11. preys:
13. threw:

Across

7. whether:
9. leek:
12. write:

8. bare:
11. principle:
14. prophet:

B Complete these using some of the commonly misused homophones.

there / they're / their	it's / its	you're / your	too / two / to
we're / were / where / wear	hear / here	are / our	know / no

1. Liam and Clara always help _____ mother with the housework.
2. "Can you _____ that noise?" asked Kilian. "_____ is it coming from?"
3. _____ impossible for most people _____ lick their elbow.
4. What _____ you going to _____ to the party tonight?
5. I have _____ sisters: Daniella and Yolanda.
6. Did you _____ that the human body is made up of sixty per cent water?
7. "Where _____ you at the time of the break in?" asked the Garda.
8. "Please leave _____ homework over _____," announced the teacher.

C In your copy, write a sentence using each of the unused words above.

Grammar – Verbs 1 – Present and Past Participles

To make **regular** present or past tense verbs, we add the present participle '**ing**' or the past participle '**ed**'. Examples:

- Short vowel sound with a consonant: double the consonant, e.g. to pin → pin**ning**, pin**ned**.
- Ending in '**e**': remove the '**e**', e.g. to race → rac**ing**, rac**ed**.
- Ending in '**ie**': change '**ie**' to '**y**' when adding '**ing**', e.g. tie → t**ying**, but ti**ed**.
- Ending in a vowel and then '**y**': add suffix, e.g. annoy → annoy**ing**, annoy**ed**.
- Ending in a consonant and then '**y**': change '**y**' to '**i**' when adding '**ed**', e.g. worry → worr**ied**, but worry**ing**.
- For most other words, just add the suffix, e.g. walk → walk**ing**, walk**ed**.

A Complete the table below.

Infinitive verb	Present participle 'ing'	Past participle 'ed'	Infinitive verb	Present participle 'ing'	Past participle 'ed'
to hop			to hurry		
to bounce			to travel		
to bully			to sway		
to lie			to scream		

B In your copy, change each present participle from section A into an adjective phrase and write it in a sentence.

Example: The **sneezing man** had run out of tissues.

Some verbs have **irregular** past participles. Instead of adding '**ed**', they may change their vowel sound and/or add other letters, e.g. to swim → swam → swum, to bite → bit → bitten.

C In your copy, complete the table below.

Infinitive verb	Simple past	Past participle	Infinitive verb	Simple past	Past participle
to write	I ...	I had ...	to shrink	she ...	she had ...
to bring	you ...	you had ...	to fall	we ...	we had ...
to hide	he ...	he had ...	to swing	they ...	they had ...

D Dictation: Listen to your teacher and write the sentences in your copy.

 I can do this!   I'm getting there.   I need help!

17

Oral Language

A You've got it all wrong!

Imagine that you are the 'baddie' in a famous story or fairytale. Convince your classmates that you did nothing wrong and the 'heroes' of the story are really to blame.

Writing Genre – Persuasive Writing

The purpose of **persuasive writing** is to present a logical argument from a particular point of view. It may be written in the form of a debate, a letter or an advertisement.

Structure:

- **Statement** – State the problem or argument. This is sometimes presented as a question.
- **Position taken** – The author gives their position (point of view) on the topic.
- **Argument** – Points arguing the position taken; the arguments 'for' are stated first, followed by the arguments 'against'.
- **Conclusion or summary** – A summary of the main points or position, an evaluation of the topic if no position was originally taken or a request for action.

A Plan, organise and write your own speech to persuade your class to vote for you in an election.

1. Choose one of the following jobs:
   - Chairperson of the student council (leader)
   - Treasurer of the student council (handles money)
   - Secretary of the student council (takes notes and keeps time in meetings)
   - Yard/sports monitor
   - Green Team leader

2. In your copy, plan your persuasive speech using a mind map like the one below.

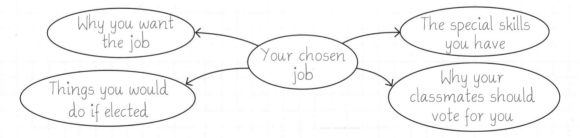

3. Use your mind map to write the first draft of your persuasive speech. Each argument should be presented in a different paragraph in the form of:
   - Point
   - Elaboration
   - Evidence

B Art activity

Design a poster to accompany your election campaign. Include a catchy slogan, your main opinions or strengths and a picture if possible.

Fairtrade: To Buy or Not to Buy?

Comprehension Strategies

A Before reading: KWL chart

Use the strategies of **Making Connections** and **Questioning**. Use the chart below to record your schema (background knowledge) on Fairtrade and anything you hope to find out from reading the text. Record what you have learned after reading.

KWL Chart		
What I know	**What I want to know**	**What I have learned**

B During reading: Fabulous five

Use the strategy of **Determining Importance**. While reading, record five key words in the text. Then, in groups, compare your 'fabulous five' and justify why you thought these were the most important words in the text.

C After reading: Debate

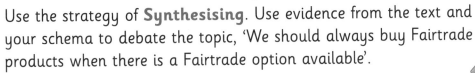

Use the strategy of **Synthesising**. Use evidence from the text and your schema to debate the topic, 'We should always buy Fairtrade products when there is a Fairtrade option available'.

Comprehension

STOP! Use your dictionary to find out the meaning of the **bold** words below.

Fairtrade: To Buy or Not to Buy?

A developing country is a country in which many people work on the land and live on very little money. Fairtrade is a way of **trading** that helps these farmers to sell their **produce** at a fair price, so that they might work their way out of **poverty**. The Fairtrade system also pays extra money, known as the Fairtrade **Premium**, to support community projects such as wells for clean water, schools and health clinics. It **encourages** safe working practices and farming methods that **improve** the environment.

FOR	AGAINST
■ It is worth paying a little more for Fairtrade produce, because you are helping to improve people's lives.	■ Fairtrade products are more expensive and shoppers on a tight **budget** cannot afford to pay extra.
■ Fairtrade helps farmers in developing countries to become **self-sufficient**.	■ Farmers can come to **depend** on the Fairtrade Premium, but what they really need is investment to make their production methods modern and **competitive**.
■ Farmers can use the Fairtrade Premium to improve the **efficiency** of their business and the quality of their produce.	■ Fairtrade only helps a small number of the **producers** who get the Fairtrade Premium. It can encourage farmers to go on growing the same crop even if prices should fall, when they would be better off switching to other crops that would sell better.
■ The Fairtrade Premium also supports community projects.	
■ Buying local produce in developed countries is not always environmentally friendly. Growing out-of-season fruit and vegetables in heated greenhouses and **polytunnels** uses fuel that creates **carbon emissions**, **contributing** to **climate change**.	■ Fairtrade produce often has to be **transported** by air to keep it fresh. This adds to 'food miles', i.e. the amount of carbon produced when food is transported, so it makes more sense to buy **locally** produced food.

Common Fairtrade products

bananas   chocolate   tea   coffee   cotton

To find out if a product is Fairtrade, just look for the sticker or symbol.

A In your copy, go investigate.

1. What is a developing country?
2. Explain the Fairtrade Premium.
3. How can Fairtrade farmers use the Fairtrade Premium to improve their business?
4. How does Fairtrade affect the environment?
5. How do developed countries grow out-of-season fruit and vegetables?
6. How would you know if a product is Fairtrade?

B In your copy, give your opinion.

1. Why do you think Fairtrade products are more expensive?
2. What do you think is the best 'for' argument?
3. What do you think is the best 'against' argument?
4. Think of at least one point to add to either the 'for' or the 'against' argument.
5. Would you buy Fairtrade having read this debate?
6. Have you ever seen or bought a Fairtrade product? What was it?

C Vocabulary

1. In groups, brainstorm all of the words you can think of to do with Fairtrade.

2. On a sheet of paper, use black, blue and green pencils or markers to draw the Fairtrade symbol. With these colours, use the words you have brainstormed to fill the Fairtrade symbol. Words can be repeated as many times as you need.

D Cloze procedure: 'Clean, Safe Water'. Fill in the blanks.

organisations   Premium   not   farmers   water   tackle   access   to   improving   pumps

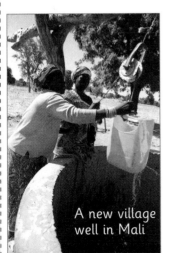

A new village well in Mali

Fairtrade is _____ just about helping people and communities.
It is also about _____ the local environment. Fairtrade
_____ work with local communities to _____
problems such as a lack of access to clean, safe _____.

Many Fairtrade _____ and growers working in regions
where _____ to water is a problem, use the Fairtrade
_____ to help pay for digging wells, installing _____
or piping clean water _____ people's homes and businesses.

Phonics – '-ance', '-ence'

'-**ance**' and '-**ence**' are suffixes added to nouns or adjectives ending in 'ant' or 'ent', or to verbs. They make abstract nouns.

Examples: **Noun** – An assistant gives assist**ance**.

Adjective – If a room is silent, there is sil**ence**.

Verb – If you guide someone, you give them guid**ance**.

A Write 'ance' or 'ence' to complete each word.

dist	audi	sequ	entr	prefer
sil	allow	bal	differ	fragr

B Match each 'ance' or 'ence' word to its root word. Tick whether the root word is a verb, a noun or an adjective.

'-ance' or '-ence' word	Root word	Verb	Noun	Adjective
1. appliance ▪	▪ deterrent			
2. existence ▪	▪ attendant			
3. disturbance ▪	▪ apply			
4. fragrance ▪	▪ fragrant			
5. eloquence ▪	▪ evident			
6. evidence ▪	▪ disturb			
7. attendance ▪	▪ exist			
8. deterrence ▪	▪ eloquent			

C Ring the correct word in each sentence.

1. My little brother is such a **nuisance** / **nuicence**.

2. "Pleased to make your **acquaintance** / **acquaintence**," said the lord.

3. Some people believe in the **existance** / **existence** of leprechauns.

4. Being student council president filled Lana with **confidance** / **confidence**.

5. The Natural History Museum of Ireland has free **admittance** / **admittence**.

6. Every room in the hotel has a hairdryer for **conveniance** / **convenience**.

Grammar – Verbs 2 – Tenses

We know that verbs come in the past, present and future tenses. They can also come in the simple, continuous and perfect tenses.

Simple tense refers to an action that has started and finished, e.g. I **walk** (present simple). For the present tense, this can also be an action that is repeated.

Continuous tense refers to an action that is still happening, e.g. I **am walking** (present continuous). Insert the irregular verb '**to be**' before the verb and add the present participle (usually '**ing**'). Remember, '**to be**' can also look like: **am**, **is**, **are**, **was**, **were**.

Perfect tense refers to an action that has been completed, e.g. I **have walked** (present perfect). Insert the irregular verb '**to have**' before the verb and add the past participle (usually '**ed**').

A Underline the verb in each sentence. Write whether it is the simple, continuous or perfect tense.

1. I will have seen this film four times by the time this is over.   Future perfect

2. Yesterday, Charli rode her bicycle home from school.   Past

3. We will be living in America next year.   Future

4. I have given my homework to my teacher every morning.   Present

5. The dog was running down the road with the stolen chicken.   Past

6. Joe and Brendan will play football all evening.   Future

7. The noise from the concert is interrupting our sleep.   Present

8. The shop had closed by the time I had arrived.   Past

9. Amir lends his Xbox games to me all the time.   Present

B In your copy, draw a large version of the table below. Using the example of 'I wrote.', fill in the verb phrases for the following:

1. She walked.   2. We clean.   3. I lift.   4. You open.   5. He reads.

6. She breathes.   7. We sing.   8. I eat.   9. They cook.   10. He hides.

	Past tense	Present tense	Future tense
Simple	I wrote.	I write.	I will write.
Continuous	I was writing.	I am writing.	I will be writing.
Perfect	I had written.	I have written.	I will have written.

C Dictation: Listen to your teacher and write the sentences in your copy.

 I can do this!   I'm getting there.   I need help!

23

Oral Language

Walking debate

Label three different areas of your classroom 'Agree', 'Not sure' and 'Disagree'. Stand in the middle of the room while your teacher reads out one of the statements below (or any other ideas you might have). Walk to the area in the room that represents how you feel about the statement. Your teacher will then pick pupils from each area to give their opinion. You are free to move if someone's argument persuades you to change your mind.

- Zoos should be shut down.
- Female sports should be more popular.
- School uniforms help to stop bullying.

Writing Genre – Persuasive Writing

The **language of persuasive writing** should include:

- nouns and pronouns that refer to general subjects, e.g. the government, nuclear power.
- technical terms, e.g. atoms, contamination.
- usually timeless present tense, e.g. pollutes, encourages (this can change if referring to the past or making predictions).
- formal objective styles, i.e. no personal pronouns. Personal opinions are presented as fact, e.g. everyone is aware that our planet is at risk.
- connectives that show cause and effect or problem and solution, that compare and contrast and show conclusion, e.g. as a result, however, therefore.

A Review, edit and rewrite your persuasive speech.

1. Make sure that your speech has all of the following:
   - Statement   - Position taken   - Arguments   - Conclusion   - Persuasive language

2. Read over your speech and edit it for spelling, punctuation and grammar.

3. Rewrite your speech and check that you have:
   - addressed your audience.
   - presented a logical and persuasive argument.

4. Check your work using the persuasive self-assessment checklist.

5. As a class, hold a mock debate using your election speeches.

B Take action: Fairtrade Fortnight

Find out when Fairtrade Fortnight falls. As a class, make an action plan to teach your school about Fairtrade, e.g. make posters, speak at assembly, try Fairtrade cooking.

The Maya

Comprehension Strategies

A Before reading: True or false?

Use the strategy of **Predicting**. Write five statements about the Maya below. Check to see if you were right after reading.

1. _____

2. _____

3. _____

4. _____

5. _____

B During reading: Tricky words

Use the strategy of **Word Attack**. Follow the steps on page vi at the beginning of the book when you come across tricky words in the text.

C During reading: Wow word wall

Use the strategy of **Word Attack**. Record your tricky words as you read and make a 'wow word wall' as a class.

D After reading: 3, 2, 1

Use the strategy of **Synthesising**.

Three things that I learned from the text:

- _____

- _____

- _____

Two interesting facts in the text:

- _____

- _____

One question that I still have:

- _____

Comprehension

 STOP! Use your dictionary to find out the meaning of the **bold** words below.

The Maya

The Maya were a great **civilisation** who lived for three thousand years from around 2,000 BC. They **resided** in the Yucatán area of Central America, which covers Guatemala, Belize and parts of Mexico, El Salvador and Honduras.

Mayan cities

The Maya never formed an **empire**. Their **society** was made up of separate large cities located in the rainforest. Each city was surrounded by smaller cities, villages and farms and had its own ruler. The cities were connected by **sturdy** roads through the jungle, which **facilitated** trade. However, the cities often fought one another. The Maya were very skilled **architects**. In each city, they built homes, palaces, temples and pyramids to worship their gods, using tools made from stone, wood or shells.

Religion

Religion was very important to the Maya. Everything they did **revolved** around pleasing their many gods. They believed that the gods watched over them and that demons from the underworld might escape and attack them if they did not **worship** in the right way. They held religious ceremonies in which priests wore masks and costumes to keep the gods happy and to scare away the demons. They also practised human **sacrifice**.

Culture

The Maya were skilled potters, weavers, artists, mathematicians and **astronomers**. They invented musical instruments, sports, chocolate and a 360-day calendar similar to the one we use today. They developed a **sophisticated** written language, made up of around 800 pictures and symbols. They used this **glyph** system to carve messages into stone and to write hundreds of books called codices, which **contained** information about history, medicine, astronomy and their religion. Unfortunately, the Spanish burned all but four of these books after they arrived in 1519 AD.

Decline of the Maya

Around 900 AD, the Maya began to **abandon** their main cultural centres of Palanque, Tikal and Copán. Historians are unsure why this happened, but suggest that war, hunger, disease, **invasion** by another civilisation or natural disasters might have played a part. Some Mayan centres continued up until the Spanish arrived.

The Maya were a historically important civilisation, who were extremely **advanced** for their time. Although we are unsure what caused their culture to decline, their **heritage** lives on in their **descendants** in Guatemala and some of its surrounding countries, and in the historians working to learn more about this great civilisation.

A In your copy, go investigate.

1. Where were the Mayan cities located?

2. What tools did the Maya use to build their cities?

3. Describe the written Mayan language.

4. What interesting things did the Maya invent?

5. In what year did the Spanish arrive in Central America?

6. Where can distant relatives of the Maya be found today?

B In your copy, give your opinion.

1. From the text, how do we know that religion was important to the Maya?

2. Why do you think it might be impressive that the Maya developed a calendar similar to the one we use today?

3. Do you agree it was unfortunate that the Spanish destroyed all but four of the Mayan codices? Why/Why not?

4. What do you think happened to the Maya of Palanque, Tikal and Copán?

5. Why do you think the author says that the Maya were very advanced for their time?

6. Would you like to have been a Maya? Explain your answer.

C Vocabulary

1. Underline the odd word out in each list below. Use your dictionary to help you.

   (a) city, metropolis, urban, capital, rural

   (b) encircled, surrounded, unfenced, enclosed, bordered

   (c) vital, optional, imperative, essential, important

   (d) regrettably, lamentably, luckily, unfortunately, grievously

   (e) mildly, immensely, utterly, extremely, overly

2. One word from each list above is found at least once in the text. Find it in the text and ring it both in the text and the list.

3. Write a sentence for each of the underlined words above.

D Cloze procedure: 'Mayan Sport'. Fill in the blanks.

The Maya were one of the first   civilization   to develop and play their own
sports   . Most Mayan cities had   their   own court dedicated to ball games.
One of the Maya's most important games was   rockball   with a rubber ball on a stone
court. The   court   was surrounded by high walls that had   spikes   attached to
the top. The   aim   of the game was to hit the ball through the hoops without using hands
or letting the   ball   hit the   hoop   . This was a very important ritual to   the
Maya. Kings and religious leaders often attended the games.

Phonics – '-ancy', '-ency'

'-**ancy**' and '-**ency**' are suffixes added to nouns, verbs or adjectives ending in 'ant' or 'ent' to make abstract nouns, e.g. vacant → vac**ancy**, urgent → urg**ency**.

A Change each noun or adjective to an abstract noun using '-ancy' or '-ency'. Underline the nouns and box the adjectives. Use your dictionary to help you.

1. infant   infancy
2. frequent
3. vibrant
4. fluent
5. consultant
6. truant
7. resident
8. pregnant
9. militant
10. tenant
11. transparent
12. proficient
13. flippant
14. coherent
15. malignant
16. consistent

B Cross out the incorrect word in each sentence.

1. Baht is the **currancy** / **currency** of Thailand.
2. I completed the test with speed and **efficiancy** / **efficiency**.
3. Our teacher has a **tendancy** / **tendency** to get distracted if we ask him questions about history.
4. There's a **discrepancy** / **discrepency** in the accounts. I haven't been paid enough.
5. Mr Balik took **redundancy** / **redundency**, because his company was failing.
6. Hassan is interested in studying **accountancy** / **accountency** in college.

C Change the words to '-ancy' or '-ency' words to complete these.

| vacant | emergent | occupant | absorbent | expectant | agent |

1. "This apartment is filthy. It is unfit for _____," said the estate agent.
2. I used a travel _____ to book my holiday to Paris.
3. There was no _____ in the hotel when we tried to book a room.
4. "Quick, call 999!" cried Sally. "There's an _____!"
5. The life _____ of a tortoise is very long.
6. The _____ of the new paper towels that Dad bought was very low.

Grammar – Commas

We use **commas** to:

- separate lists of nouns, adjectives and actions in a sentence,
  e.g. I like to eat carrots, strawberries and sandwiches for my lunch.

- separate speech from the rest of the sentence,
  e.g. "It's my turn," said Jasmine. Harry asked Andrew, "Can I please borrow your ruler?"

- separate a person's name in a sentence when directly addressing them,
  e.g. I am writing, Kevin, to remind you that your library books are overdue.

A Rewrite these in your copy, inserting commas where necessary.

1. "Please hand me the hammer nails and screwdriver" said the builder.

2. "When you get to my house, we can play computer games bake cookies watch television and play chasing with my neighbours" said Diane excitedly.

3. The strong graceful black horse raced around the field.

4. "You should always start a sentence with a capital letter Olivia" said the teacher.

5. The dog ran around chased a squirrel and dug a hole in the garden.

6. I have long curly black hair, but my sister has short straight blonde hair.

7. "Come over here Emily I have something to show you" announced Cian.

Commas can also be used to connect sentences with the words 'when', 'if', 'although', 'as', 'unless', 'after', 'while' and 'since', e.g. I like to read. I don't like newspapers. →
Although I like to read, I don't like newspapers.

B Use the underlined words above and a comma to complete these.

1. _____ you like chocolate you will love the cake my mother made.

2. _____ Jack is very tall he could not reach the top shelf.

3. _____ Fionn was younger he liked to play with his teddies.

4. _____ I was cleaning my room my big sister was mopping the floor.

5. " _____ you finish your carrots you are not having any dessert," said Dad.

6. _____ I get home from school I change my clothes.

7. _____ Natalie walked to school she looked at the beautiful flowers.

8. _____ Danny was very young he has enjoyed swimming.

C Dictation: Listen to your teacher and write the sentences in your copy.

I can do this!   I'm getting there.   I need help!

Oral Language

A Don't say it!

Text-specific vocabulary is important when writing reports. In pairs, practise this skill by playing 'Don't say it'. Pupil A describes an object/person/place to their partner without using its name, e.g. "Used to process and store information. Made up of a CPU and a screen. Gigabytes and hard drive are some of the terms associated with it." ... A computer! Once pupil B guesses correctly, swap roles.

Writing Genre – Report Writing

The purpose of **report writing** is to present factual information to the reader.

Structure:

- **Classification** (introduction) – In the form of a definition or a short description. Give a general overview and save the details for later.
- **Description** – A detailed description of the topic using sub-headings. Try to make the sub-headings clever or funny to draw your reader's attention.
- **Summarising comment** (conclusion) – Can include an impersonal comment evaluating the topic.
- **Other** – A labelled diagram, a fact box or a glossary (a dictionary with subject-specific vocabulary).

A Plan, organise and write a report about a civilisation of your choice.

1. Choose your civilisation. Examples could include the Egyptians, the Incas, Native Americans, the Romans or any other civilisation that interests you.

2. You will need to research your civilisation using the internet or books. In your copy, draw a mind map like the template below. Each civilisation has different important information, so decide on the best topics to write about from your research and include them in your mind map. For example:

3. Using the information in your mind map, write the first draft of your report. Remember to include interesting information to inform and entertain your reader.

B Art activity

Use the internet to research ancient Mayan art with your teacher. Then, create ceremonial Mayan mosaic masks with cut-up squares of paper on a large piece of card. Use two or three bright colours and some tinfoil or gold paper if you can.

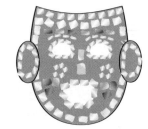

The Skin

6

Comprehension Strategies

A Before reading: Before, during, after reading

Use the strategy of **Questioning**. Record any questions you have …

Before reading	During reading	After reading

B During reading: Turn on the lights!

Use the strategy of **Clarifying**. Stop and notice when you have a a 'lightbulb moment'. This is when something in the text is clarified or explained. Record your lightbulb moments below.

C After reading: Fact or fib?

Use the strategy of **Synthesising**. Write three facts and one fib about the text. Then, in pairs, swap your lists and find each other's fib.

1. _____

2. _____

3. _____

4. _____

D After reading: Beat the buzzer

Use the strategy of **Questioning** and the skill of **Skimming**. Write a question about the text on a post-it. Your teacher can collect all of the questions and ask them of the class one by one. You must then skim the text to locate the exact line that gives the answer. When you have found it, press the buzzer (i.e. call out your name) to answer.

Comprehension

 STOP! Use your dictionary to find out the meaning of the **bold** words below.

The Skin

The skin is the largest organ in the body. It is **comprised** of three layers: the epidermis, the dermis and the subcutaneous fat.

The epidermis

The epidermis is the outer layer of the skin. It is made up of cells that are **produced** at the bottom of the epidermis. It takes them about four weeks to reach the **surface**, where they die and get replaced. The body is **constantly shedding** dead skin cells and making new ones to replace them.

The epidermis also **contains** melanin. The more melanin a person has, the darker their skin is. Melanin protects us from the sun. However, it needs to be helped by wearing sun cream.

Diagram labels: Sweat gland · Pore · Nerve endings · Hair follicle · Arrector pili · Epidermis · Dermis · Subcutaneous fat · Oil gland · Blood vessels

The dermis

The dermis contains blood vessels and nerve endings. Nerve endings send messages to the brain through the nervous system. The nerve endings in the dermis tell the brain about the things we touch. This is very important, as the brain then tells us how to **react** to what we've touched, such as moving away from something hot.

The dermis also contains oil glands and sweat glands. Oil glands create sebum, an oily **substance** that moves to the surface of the skin and creates an oily layer to **moisten** and protect the skin. Sweat glands create sweat, which also moves to the epidermis and is released from tiny holes called pores. Sweat helps us to keep cool.

This layer of the skin also contains hair follicles, where hair begins to grow. Hair follicles are **connected** to arrector pili. These are tiny muscles that **contract** when we are cold, making our hair stand up and causing goose bumps.

The blood vessels in the dermis narrow when we are cold to keep the blood away from the cool surface of the skin. In **addition** to this, they widen when we are hot to bring the blood closer to the surface and help us to cool down.

The subcutaneous fat

Subcutaneous fat helps to keep us warm and protects our bones and organs.

The skin is often an **overlooked** organ. However, the many vital jobs it performs makes it one of the most important organs in the body.

Glossary

Brain: A large organ that controls the body and the mind

Cells: The building blocks of living things, which carry out important jobs for the body

Nervous system: Controls all actions in the body

Blood vessel: A small tube that carries blood around the body

A **In your copy, go investigate.**

1. What is the largest organ of the body?

2. Name the three layers of the skin.

3. Where are skin cells produced?

4. What can be found in the dermis?

5. Why is sweat important?

6. How does the skin react to the cold?

B **In your copy, give your opinion.**

1. Name at least three things you can do to protect your skin.

2. Why is it important for the skin and the brain to work together?

3. What other feelings do you think the skin can detect?

4. What do you think is the most important function of the skin?

5. Why does the author say that the skin is one of the most important organs in the body?

6. Do you agree with the author about the importance of the skin? Why/Why not?

C **Vocabulary: Look back over the text and explain what the following parts of the skin do.**

1. Melanin: _____

2. Nerve endings: _____

3. Oil glands: _____

4. Subcutaneous fat: _____

5. Arrector pili: _____

D **Cloze procedure: 'Sports Day'. Fill in the blanks.**

It was sports day and Lara was getting _____ to compete in the girls' 400 m sprint final. "On your marks, get set, ____ !" The whistle blew and Lara shot away _____ her starting point. Tracy McGuire was just _____ of her, but Lara pushed herself as hard _____ she could and passed her as they sprinted over the _____ line. Lara had won! She was so happy that she could hardly contain herself, until Tracy and _____ friends began to _____ at her. "Look everyone! Lara's got a red face and sweat patches on her T-shirt!" Lara was so _____. She felt her face getting redder and redder. "Don't be silly, girls," said Mrs Burns, the PE teacher. "That's just the body's way of naturally _____ itself down. You all have _____ on your T-shirts. Your faces are turning _____ now too." Lara couldn't help but smile as she received her _____. She wasn't so sure that the other girls' faces _____ red because they had been running.

Phonics – Prefixes 'multi-', 'mono-', 'mega-', 'micro-'

Prefixes are letters added to the beginning of words that change their meaning.

'**multi-**' means many, e.g. **multi**ply.

'**mono-**' means one, e.g. **mono**rail.

'**mega-**' means great or big, e.g. **mega**watt. In measurements, 'mega-' means one million.

'**micro-**' means small or tiny, e.g. **micro**wave. In measurements, 'micro-' means one millionth.

A Split each 'multi-', 'mono-', 'mega-' or 'micro-' word into its prefix and root word. Write the meaning using the root word as a clue. Check your answers using a dictionary. ✏️

Word	Prefix	Root word	My meaning	Dictionary check
1. multinational				
2. monotone				
3. megaphone				
4. microbiology				
5. megastar				
6. multipurpose				
7. microchip				
8. monosyllabic				

B Use the correct prefix to complete the words in these sentences. ✏️

1. I made a _____ coloured tie-dye T-shirt in my art class last week.

2. The _____ biologist uses a _____ scope to investigate _____ organisms.

3. On our school tour, we visited a _____ lith that was built thousands of years ago.

4. The rich man wore a _____ cle instead of glasses to the theatre.

5. Vid is _____ talented. He plays the violin, sings and cooks very well.

6. A _____ watt is one million units of electricity.

7. My sister always wins when our family plays _____ poly.

8. Danils wore traditional Ukrainian clothes to the _____ cultural night in school.

C Write sentences using some of the 'multi-', 'mono-', 'mega-' and 'micro-' words above. Choose a number to challenge yourself. ✏️

Grammar – Singular and Plural

Singular means one. **Plural** means more than one.

- For most words, just add an 's', e.g. table → table**s**.
- Words ending in a consonant and then 'y': change 'y' to 'ies', e.g. balcony → balcon**ies**.
- Words ending in 's', 'x', 'z', 'sh', 'ch', 'ss' or a consonant plus 'o': add 'es', e.g. box → box**es**.
- Words ending in 'f' or 'fe': remove the 'f' or 'fe' and add 'ves', e.g. loaf → loa**ves**.
- Some words are irregular, e.g. fish → fish, child → children.

A Complete this table of singular and plural nouns.

Singular	Plural	Singular	Plural	Singular	Plural
couch		compass			deer
	buzzes		buffaloes	army	
alley		wife			knives
	butterflies		these	hero	

When changing a noun in a sentence to plural, it is important to remember that other words such as pronouns and verbs might need to change too, e.g. The dog chases the cat every day. → The dog**s** **chase** the cat**s** every day.

Top tip!

a flower → (some) flowers

the flower → the flowers

that flower → those flowers

this flower → these flowers

B In your copy, rewrite these sentences, changing the nouns to plural.

Tip: Make sure the pronouns and verbs agree.

1. The army has come to my town.
2. The girl plays with her new doll after school.
3. She keeps her fish in a fishbowl.
4. This child is looking for his dad.
5. That fox likes to chase deer.
6. The man's wife lost her glasses.

C In your copy, correct these sentences in the plural.

1. My tooth are very sore.
2. The shelf in my bedroom are about to fall down.
3. This radishes tastes delicious.
4. The men is wearing his boots.
5. We are having those potato for my dinner.

D Dictation: Listen to your teacher and write the sentences in your copy.

I can do this! 　I'm getting there. 　I need help!

Oral Language

A Dictionary game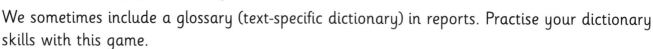

We sometimes include a glossary (text-specific dictionary) in reports. Practise your dictionary skills with this game.

> Divide the class into two teams: the red team and the blue team. The teacher draws a 5 × 5 grid on the board and writes the letters of the alphabet randomly in each box, excluding x, y and z. The teams must pick a letter to start. The teacher then reads the definition of a word beginning with that letter from a dictionary. If the team names the word correctly, they must colour that square using their team colour. If they guess incorrectly, the other team can guess the word without interrupting their own turn. The aim of the game is to colour three squares in a row. Teams may block each other to gain an advantage.

Writing Genre – Report Writing

The **language of a report** should include:

- general subjects, e.g. the Maya, they, it, the skin.
- impersonal objective language, i.e. first-person pronouns (I, my, etc.) and opinions are not included.
- timeless present tense.
- subject-specific vocabulary, e.g. subtropical, epidermis, habitat.
- factual, precise adjectives, e.g. oily substance.
- words for classifying, defining, comparing and contrasting, e.g. were named, belong to, are similar to, were weaker than.

A Review, edit and rewrite your civilisation report.

1. Make sure that your report has all of the following:
   - Clarification
   - Description
   - A summarising comment (conclusion)
   - Report language

2. Read over your report and edit it for spelling, punctuation, grammar and relevant information.

3. Rewrite your report and include the following:
   - A labelled diagram
   - A fact box
   - A glossary
   - A border of important images related to your civilisation

4. Check your work using the report self-assessment checklist.

B Debate: 'Using sun cream is pointless in Ireland.'

Comprehension Strategies

A Before reading: I wonder …

Use the strategy of **Questioning**. Fill in the thought bubbles with questions about the text.

I wonder
_____
_____
_____

I wonder
_____
_____
_____

I wonder
_____
_____
_____

B During reading: Five senses

Use the strategy of **Visualising**. Look at the painting and imagine that you are one of the characters. Record what you can see, hear, smell, taste and touch.

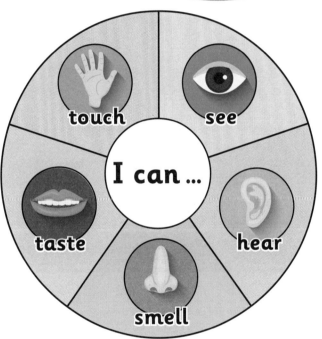

touch • see

I can …

taste • hear

smell

C During reading

Use the strategy of **Clarifying**. We need something clarified when we read a word, a phrase or an idea that we don't understand. Here are some steps to help you clarify:

- Read back.
- Read on.
- Think of your schema. Do you have any background knowledge that might help?
- Is there any information in the image/s that might help?
- Might another phrase make sense here?

D After reading: Interview

Use the strategy of **Inferring**. In your copy, make a list of interview questions that you would ask Vincent van Gogh or one of the characters in the painting. In pairs, answer each other's questions using evidence from the painting and text.

Comprehension

 Use your dictionary to find out the meaning of the **bold** words below.

'The Potato Eaters'

By Vincent van Gogh (painted during April–May 1885)

Vincent van Gogh was a Dutch artist who lived in the 1800s. Van Gogh painted many famous paintings such as '*Starry Night*', '*Sunflowers*' and '*Bedroom in Arles*' along with numerous self-portraits and landscapes. He is known for his use of **vivid** colour, **broad** brushstrokes and **emotive** subject matter. '*The Potato Eaters*' was van Gogh's first **major** work. At the time, he had not yet begun to use the **vibrant** colours that his paintings are now known for. His early paintings mainly **consisted** of the dark tones used above.

Van Gogh chose **coarse** and ugly models in order to **represent** the **peasant subjects** naturally: "You see, I really have wanted to make it so that people get the idea that these folk, who are eating their potatoes by the light of their little lamp, have tilled the earth themselves with these hands they are putting in the dish, and so it speaks of manual labour and that they have thus honestly earned their food. I wanted it to give the idea of a wholly different way of life from ours – civilised people. So I certainly don't want everyone just to admire it or approve of it without knowing why."

A In your copy, go investigate.

1. What are the people in this painting doing? What tells you this?
2. Are there any children in the painting? How do you know?
3. What is the woman on the right doing?
4. Describe their clothes. Why are they wearing clothes like these?
5. What kind of a home do these people live in?
6. Are these people rich or poor? How do you know?

B In your copy, give your opinion.

1. Why did van Gogh choose 'ugly' models?
2. Do you think the colours of the painting suit the subject? Why?
3. What do you think van Gogh meant by the underlined quote?
4. What do you think the atmosphere is like in this home? Explain.
5. Can you think of another title for this painting?
6. Do you like this painting? Why/Why not?

C Vocabulary

Unscramble each word from the text and match it to its meaning.

(i) eevoitm: _____   **(ii)** lidisciev: _____   **(iii)** nrtiavb: _____

(iv) amerdi: _____   **(v)** donstcsie: _____   **(vi)** npstaesa: _____

(a) To look at something with pleasure or respect   _____

(b) Composed (made up) of   _____

(c) Causing strong emotions for or against something   _____

(d) Polite and well mannered   _____

(e) People living in extremely poor conditions   _____

(f) Bright and colourful   _____

D Cloze procedure: 'Vincent van Gogh'. Fill in the blanks.

Vincent van Gogh was _____ in the Netherlands in 1853. He drew as a child, but did not _____ to paint until his late twenties. He was a thoughtful man and battled with mental illness, which many believe influenced his _____. One of his most _____ paintings is a self-portrait showing a bandage covering his partly cut-off ear. He is known for painting with _____ colours and broad _____ and is famous for works such as 'Sunflowers' and '_____ Night'. Most of his best-known works were completed in the last two years of his _____. Critics mostly ignored _____ work until his death in 1890, but his paintings are now some of the most _____ ever sold.

Phonics – '-ary', '-ery', '-ory'

'**-ary**', '**-ery**' and '**-ory**' are different sounds, but they are very similar and are often mixed up, e.g. diction**ary**, cel**ery**, access**ory**.

A Complete each word using '-ary', '-ery' or '-ory'.

secret	hist	cutl	arch
batt	libr	surg	vict
iv	imagin	categ	Febru

B Complete each word and match it to its meaning.

g_ll_ry   s_l_t_ry   _bs_rv_t_ry   fl_tt_ry   _nn_v_rs_ry   m_m_ry

1. The mental faculty or act of retaining information

2. A yearly celebration, often of marriage

3. A building in which works of art are displayed or sold

4. The act of complementing another

5. A building dedicated to studying the planets and stars

6. To be or live alone

C Ring the correct word in each sentence.

1. The scientist celebrated his **discovary** / **discovery** in his **laboratory** / **laboratery**.

2. I have green eyes and so does Mum. Mum says that it's **hereditary** / **hereditory**.

3. Maths is a **compulsary** / **compulsory** subject in **secondary** / **secondery** school.

4. Dad uses a lot of dangerous **machinery** / **machinary** on the farm.

5. It is **necessery** / **necessary** to report a **robbery** / **robbary**.

6. Our **conservatory** / **conservatery** gets very hot in the summer.

7. When Shamika won the **lottery** / **lottory**, she bought an **extraordinary** / **extraordinery** new house.

Grammar – The Apostrophe

The **apostrophe** is used to show that letters have been removed from shortened words. These are called contractions, e.g. should have → should've (NOT 'should of'), it will → it'll.

A In your copy, rewrite these using contractions where possible.

1. "You should not eat too much sugar. It will damage your teeth," said the dentist.

2. "It is such a beautiful day that I am sure they will enjoy the park," said Karl.

3. Patricia would have walked to the shop if she had known it was so close.

4. "It is not very cold today, so I might not bring my coat," thought Cian.

5. Paulina would not like to visit the beach, because she does not like sand.

6. I cannot help you with your homework. You will have to do it yourself.

7. "What has happened to the mice?" asked Maria. "They have disappeared," replied Luca.

The **apostrophe** can also be used to show ownership.
For a single owner, we add **'s** to the end of the word, e.g. the cat**'s** tail.
For a single owner ending in '**s**', the rule is the same, e.g. James**'s** house.
For a plural owner ending in '**s**', just add an apostrophe after the '**s**', e.g. the boys' jumpers.
For an irregular plural owner not ending in '**s**', add **'s**, e.g. the men**'s** coats.

B Rewrite these with an apostrophe.

1. The toys belonging to the girls _____the girls' toys_____

2. The worm belonging to the bird 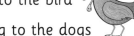 _____

3. The puppies belonging to the dogs _____

4. The children belonging to the women _____

5. The wheels belonging to the bus _____

6. The legs belonging to the chairs _____

7. The principal belonging to the school _____

8. The tails belonging to the monkeys _____

C In your copy, write some sentences using the apostrophe to show contractions and ownership. Pick a number to challenge yourself.

D Dictation: Listen to your teacher and write the sentences in your copy.

I can do this!   I'm getting there.   I need help!

41

Oral Language

A Tongue-twisters

In pairs, create a list of rhyming or alliterative (beginning consonants sounding the same) words. Arrange them together to create a silly tongue-twister. Write your tongue-twister down and challenge other pairs to say it as fast as they can without tripping over their words. Examples:

- How much wood would a woodchuck chuck if a woodchuck could chuck wood?
- She sells seashells by the seashore.

Writing Genre – Poetry Writing

A poem is a fictional text written to entertain the reader. Poetry manipulates and arranges words to create unique perspectives on the world. The poet combines words and imagery in order to share personal thoughts and feelings about a subject.

Haiku

A haiku is a traditional Japanese poem that often doesn't rhyme or have a title. It captures a moment of beauty, an element of nature or an important experience. The first two lines are related and the third line reveals something surprising, while still being connected to the first two. Emotion is portrayed by describing the event that caused emotion without describing the emotion itself. Below are the rules for writing a haiku, along with an example.

1st line: five syllables	A short walk to home
2nd line: seven syllables	Leaves sway gently in the breeze
3rd line: five syllables	Home alone again

A Write some haikus of your own.

- Try to write from experience.
- Include some mention of nature or the season if possible.
- Use descriptions related to the senses.
- Evoke an emotion by describing what caused the emotion.

B Drama: Set the scene

Tableau: In groups, create the scene from 'The Potato Eaters'. Use props if possible. Think carefully about your character: how they look, what they are doing, how they are feeling and what they are thinking. Show your scene to the class in a carousel (every group is ready at the same time in different areas of the room and the teacher asks the groups to show their tableau, one at a time).

Thought tracking: The teacher can walk through each group, tapping pupils on the shoulder and inviting them to share their character's thoughts.

Revision and Assessment 8

Revision: Grammar and Phonics

Look back at the grammar on pages 5, 11, 17, 23, 29, 35 and 41.

Day 1

1. Ring for capital letters and add the punctuation.
   - (a) does clara learn german on mondays
   - (b) wow theres the statue of liberty

2. Tick for the underlined noun.
   - (a) I feel <u>calm</u> when I listen to music.

     Concrete   Abstract

     Collective
   - (b) There is a <u>pride</u> of lions over there.

     Concrete   Abstract

     Collective
   - (c) The <u>fire</u> blazed through the night.

     Concrete   Abstract

     Collective

3. Insert commas.
   - (a) "Are you hungry Nigel?" asked Pat.
   - (b) Although it is sunny I am cold.

4. Rewrite with an apostrophe.

   the toys belonging to the boys

   _____

5. Rewrite as plural.
   - (a) that box _____
   - (b) this hero _____

6. Ring the silent letter.
   - (a) thumb (b) campaign (c) receipt

7. Tick the correct word.

   I will _____ my clothes after school.

   singe   change   plunge

Day 2

1. Ring for capital letters and add the punctuation.
   - (a) we love christmas said mr murphy
   - (b) i will be in india in april may and june

2. Tick two boxes for the underlined verb.
   - (a) Rebecca <u>is playing</u> the piano.

     Past   Present

     Simple   Continuous
   - (b) She <u>will have walked</u> away by then.

     Present   Future

     Perfect   Continuous

3. Insert commas.
   - (a) It's my turn now said Ciara.
   - (b) Louis Sara and Lisa are here.

4. Rewrite with an apostrophe.

   the coats belonging to the men

   _____

5. Rewrite as plural.
   - (a) a child _____
   - (b) the army _____

6. Ring the correct spelling.
   - (a) distence / distance
   - (b) preference / preferance
   - (c) currency / currancy

7. Insert the correct prefix: multi-, mono-, mega-, micro-
   - (a) _____rail (b) _____scope
   - (c) _____lith (d) _____coloured

Revision: Grammar and Phonics

Day 3

1. Tick for the underlined noun.

   (a) The <u>band</u> of thieves were arrested.

   Concrete ☐   Abstract ☐

   Collective ☐

   (b) They sang with <u>enthusiasm</u>.

   Concrete ☐   Abstract ☐

   Collective ☐

   (c) The <u>postman</u> has lost our letters.

   Concrete ☐   Abstract ☐

   Collective ☐

2. Add the present (ing) and past (ed) participles.

Verb	Present	Past
stay		
worry		
lie		
dream		
win		

3. Insert commas.

   (a) So Adi tell me what happened.

   (b) Unless she is going I'm not going.

4. Change to nouns with '-ance' or '-ence'.

   (a) relevant: _____

   (b) evident: _____

   (c) fragrant: _____

   (d) eloquent: _____

5. Ring the correct homophone.

   (a) Can I buy some stationary / stationery?

   (b) The cat has hurt it's / its tail.

   (c) I have a sister too / two / to.

Day 4

1. Ring for capital letters and add the punctuation.

   (a) can we watch *home and away* now

   (b) i have polish english and greek friends

   (c) hey my birthday is in january too

2. Tick two boxes for the underlined verb.

   (a) Eimear <u>will go</u> to school tomorrow.

   Past ☐   Future ☐

   Simple ☐   Perfect ☐

   (b) We <u>were walking</u> to the shop.

   Past ☐   Present ☐

   Simple ☐   Continuous ☐

3. Rewrite with apostrophes.

   (a) should have   _____

   (b) Jamess house   _____

   (c) the horses manes   _____

4. Rewrite as plural.

   (a) that sheep   _____

   (b) this tooth   _____

5. Change to nouns with '-ancy' or '-ency'.

   (a) truant: _____

   (b) resident: _____

   (c) transparent: _____

   (d) malignant: _____

6. Ring the correct spelling.

   (a) archery / archory

   (b) victery / victory

   (c) secretary / secretery

7. Ring the silent letter.

   (a) aunt   **(b)** wrestler

   (c) folks   **(d)** column

Assessment: Phonics

A Ring the correct spelling.

1. A **dictionary** / **dictionery** can be used to find the synonym of a word.

2. I would like to study **accountancy** / **accountency** in college.

3. The villain got his **revenje** / **revenge**.

4. "Ugh, you are such a **nuisance** / **nuisence**," huffed Isobel to her brother.

5. **Celery** / **Celary** is a very healthy vegetable, as it is full of vitamins.

6. "Quick, come help me," said the trapped man with **urgancy** / **urgency**.

7. Dina won her dance competition in the overall **category** / **categary**.

8. The **audience** / **audiance** gave a standing ovation after the opera.

8

B Insert the correct homophone.

1. Our school earned _____ first Green Flag today. **its** / **it's**

2. A female _____ is called a doe. **dear** / **deer**

3. My favourite _____ is cornflakes. **serial** / **cereal**

4. I love _____ scarf. It's beautiful. **you're** / **your**

5. I am going to _____ a Christmas card to my nan. **right** / **write**

6. Sandra likes _____ go swimming in the summer. **too** / **to** / **two**

7. Our _____ has an office near the front door. **principal** / **principle**

8. _____ are thirteen loaves in a baker's dozen. **there** / **their** / **they're**

8

C Ring the silent letter.

1. knight	2. column	3. doubt	4. aunt	5. chalk
6. wring	7. gnu	8. hours	9. pneumonia	10. foreign

10

D Write the correct prefix: 'multi-', 'mono-', 'mega-' or 'micro-'.

1. _____ply	2. _____national	3. _____watt	4. _____wave

4

E Change to abstract nouns using the correct suffix.

-ance or -ence		-ancy or -ency	
attendant		consultant	
evident		proficient	
disturb		absorbent	
exist		occupant	

8

45

Assessment: Comprehension

Festivals of Light

There are many different religions around the world, most of which hold festivals to celebrate their history or stories. In several religions, light is an important symbol of goodness and so festivals of light are common. During these festivals, religious followers light lamps and candles to celebrate.

Diwali

Diya

Diwali is also known as 'the festival of lights', as the word 'Diwali' means 'a row of lights'. Diwali is a Hindu festival that is celebrated in October or November. The festival lasts for five days. Hindus clean their homes and decorate them with colourful *rangoli* patterns and little clay lamps called *diyas*. The festival celebrates the return of Rama and Sita and the lamps are placed in windows to guide their way home. Hindus also believe that the goddess Lakshmi will enter a beautiful, clean home and bless those who live there with wealth and happiness for the year to come. Hindus light fireworks, dress up in new clothes, visit relatives and exchange cards and gifts.

Hanukkah

Menorah

Hanukkah is the Jewish festival of light, which takes place in November or December. It celebrates the defeat of the Greeks who destroyed a temple in Jerusalem. After the temple was repaired, an oil lamp was lit. The oil should only have lasted for one day, but lasted for eight. This was known as the Miracle of the Oil. Hanukkah is a time for celebrating with family. The most important ritual of the festival is the lighting of one candle on a *menorah* (a special nine-branched candlestick) each night for eight nights. Children play a game with a spinning top called a *dreidel*, and *latkes*, potato pancakes fried in oil, are eaten.

Christmas

Christmas candles

Christmas is a Christian celebration. In the weeks leading up to Christmas, advent candles are lit to mark the countdown to Christmas. On Christmas Eve, December 24th, some people place candles in their window to guide Joseph and Mary while they look for a place for Mary to give birth to the baby Jesus. Many Christians decorate trees with lights and some place a star on top. This commemorates the star that helped the Three Wise Men to find their way to Jesus after his birth. A big meal is eaten on Christmas Day and gifts are exchanged to remember the gifts that the Three Wise Men brought to Jesus.

Assessment: Comprehension and Vocabulary

A **In your copy, go investigate.**

1. Pick one of the festivals and explain how it is celebrated in your own words.

2. What do Hindus hope will happen if they clean their homes and decorate them with lights?

3. Why do you think lighting the *menorah* is the most important ritual of Hanukkah?

4. What do you think is significant about the way that *latkes* are cooked?

5. What similarities do you see in these festivals?

6. Which festival do you think sounds the most fun or interesting? Why?

☐ 6

B **Vocabulary: Match each word with its meaning.**

melanin	produce	utter	essential	vibrant	poverty

1. Lively, exciting, bright and colourful

2. To make or manufacture

3. Extreme lack of money, goods or support

4. To speak

5. Pigment found in the skin that effects its colour

6. Absolutely necessary

☐ 6

C **Cloze procedure: 'The Snow Queen'. Fill in the blanks.**

Once, an evil goblin made a horrid mirror _____ reflected the world as an ugly and bad place. One day, the mirror broke and shards of it travelled across the land. Some of the pieces _____ to the village were Kay and Gerda lived. They were a brother and _____ who loved each other dearly. The shards of mirror lodged _____ in Kay's heart. Suddenly, Kay became mean to Gerda, teasing her and hitting _____ whenever he got the chance. One _____, when Kay was playing in the snow, a carriage stopped and its beautiful occupant beckoned _____ inside. It was the wicked Snow Queen, dressed in white furs with a _____ of ice resting on her head. She took Kay to her ice palace, where he stayed, because his heart had become poisoned _____ the mirror. Gerda _____ devastated and set out to rescue Kay. When she came upon him in the ice _____, she ran to embrace him, her tears of relief dropping onto his chest. Suddenly, warmed by Gerda's _____, Kay's heart began to thaw. He realised his mistake in choosing to live with the _____ Queen and he and Gerda escaped the palace together.

☐ 13

Assessment: Grammar

A In each of the sentences below:

1. Ring the words that need a capital letter and add the missing punctuation.

2. Find a noun and a verb.

3. Write the question number in the appropriate place in the tense table.

Capital letters ⬜ 11

(a) i have performed with enthusiasm in all of my dance shows

Punctuation ⬜ 9

(b) will you be going to see *the hunger games* in the cinema   asked tina

(c) every summer, I visit my cousins lily daisy and rose in new york

Noun	Verb

⬜ 6

Tense:	Past	Present	Future
Simple			
Continuous			
Perfect			

⬜ 3

B Ring the mistake/s in each sentence.

1. The woman found the girls's boxes.

2. I cant see the eiffel tower from my hotel room in paris.

3. "We are walked to school now", said Zack.

4. I should of gone to the beach with my friend Caroline Amy and Josh.

⬜ 10

C Change each sentence to plural.

1. This child is fast. _____

2. The hero lost his cape. _____

3. That fly chases the light. _____

4. This knife cuts well. _____

⬜ 4

D Write the verb phrases correctly in the table.

	Past tense to sing (I)	Present tense to lie (we)	Future tense to win (she)
Simple			
Continuous			
Perfect			

⬜ 9

E Dictation: Listen to your teacher and write the sentences in your copy.

| I can do this! 👍 ⬤ | I'm getting there. ✊ ⬤ | I need help! 🚩 ⬤ |

Shmuel's Story

9

Comprehension Strategies

A Before reading: Changing images

Use the strategy of **Visualising**. In your copy, draw a picture to show what you can picture before, during and after reading.

B During reading: This reminds me of ...

Use the strategy of **Making Connections**. As you read, mark places in the text where you make connections with:

Yourself	Another text	The outside world
"This reminds me of a time I …"	"This reminds me of something I read …" "The character … reminds me of … because …"	"This reminds me of what I know about …" "Knowing about … helped me to understand this text because …"

C After reading: Story map

Use the strategies of **Summarising** and **Determining Importance**. Complete the story map. Are you left with any questions?

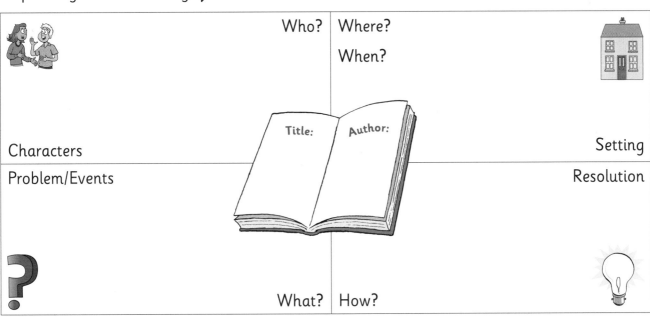

Who?   Where?
When?

Characters   Setting

Problem/Events   Resolution

Title: Author:

?

What?   How?

D After reading: Rating scale

Use the strategy of **Inferring**. In pairs, rate Bruno and Shmuel's character traits on the scale below. Justify your answers with evidence from the text

Character traits: good/bad, selfish/selfless, kind/mean, strong/weak, brave/cowardly
Rating scale: very, a little, not sure, not at all

Comprehension

Use your dictionary to find out the meaning of the **bold** words below.

Shmuel's Story

"That happened to me too!" shouted Bruno, **delighted** that he wasn't the only boy who'd been forced to move [...]

"When we were told we couldn't live in our house, we had to move to a different part of Cracow, where the soldiers built a big wall and my mother and father and my brother and I all had to live in one room … Then one day the soldiers all came with huge trucks," continued Shmuel [...] "And everyone was told to leave the houses. Lots of people didn't want to and they hid wherever they could find a place, but in the end I think they caught everyone. And the trucks took us to a train and the train …" He **hesitated** for a moment and bit his lip. Bruno thought he was going to start crying and couldn't understand why.

"The train was horrible," said Shmuel. "There were too many of us in the **carriages** for one thing. And there was no air to breathe. And it smelled awful."

"That's because you all **crowded** onto one train," said Bruno, remembering the two trains he had seen at the station when he left Berlin. "When we came here, there was another one on the other side of the **platform**, but no one seemed to see it. That was the one we got. You should have got on to it too."

"I don't think we would have been allowed," said Shmuel, shaking his head. "We weren't able to get out of our carriage."

"The doors are at the end," explained Bruno.

"There weren't any doors," said Shmuel.

"Of course there were doors," said Bruno with a sigh.
"They're at the end," he repeated. "Just past the **buffet** section."

"There weren't any doors," insisted Shmuel. "If there had been, we would have got off."

Bruno **mumbled** something under his breath along the lines of "Of course there were," but he didn't say it very loud, so Shmuel didn't hear.

"When the train finally stopped," continued Shmuel, "we were in a very cold place and we all had to walk here."

"We had a car," said Bruno, out loud now.

"And Mama was taken away from us, and Papa and Josef and I were put into the huts over there and that's where we've been ever since."

Shmuel looked very sad when he told this story and Bruno didn't know why; it didn't seem like such a terrible thing to him, and after all, much the same thing had happened to him.

(From *'The Boy in the Striped Pyjamas'* by John Boyne)

A In your copy, go investigate.

1. Why was Bruno happy at the beginning of Shmuel's story?

2. What did people do to try to escape the soldiers?

3. Where was Bruno's old home?

4. Why didn't Shmuel and his family get off their train?

5. Describe either Bruno or Shmuel's journey to this place.

6. What kind of home does Shmuel live in now?

B In your copy, give your opinion.

1. Why do you think Shmuel has to pause before he describes his train journey?

2. How were Bruno and Shmuel's journeys different and how were they similar?

3. Why do you think their journeys were so different?

4. Does Bruno understand Shmuel's story completely? Why do you think this is so?

5. Pick a part of Shmuel's story and describe how you would feel in that situation.

6. Compare Bruno and Shmuel's personalities. What are their differences and similarities?

C Vocabulary

1. Write 'true' or 'false' for each of the following statements.

    (a) Food was served on Bruno's train.

    (b) Shmuel cries as he tells his story.

    (c) Bruno and Shmuel had to leave their homes.

    (d) There are three members in Shmuel's family.

    (e) Bruno was forced to move to Cracow.

    (f) Shmuel lives with his mother now.

    (g) The doors of Bruno's train were at the end.

    (h) There were a lot of people on Shmuel's train.

2. In your copy, write a number of the bold words from the text in sentences. Choose a number to challenge yourself. Use your dictionary to help you.

D Cloze procedure: *'The Boy in the Striped Pyjamas'*. Fill in the blanks.

Nine-year-   Bruno is unaware of the horrors   country is forcing upon the Jewish people of Europe. All   is concerned with is the boring new house he has been forced to   to from his beloved home in Berlin. Bruno is fed up with the lack of friends and things to do and so   to do some exploring of the desolate area in which he now finds   . Beyond the walls of his garden, Bruno   a fence enclosing a strange camp,   all the campers wear the same uniform of striped   . It is here that Bruno meets Shmuel, a   the same age as him in a very different circumstance.

Phonics – '-sure', '-ture'

'-**sure**' and '-**ture**' are different sounds, but they are very similar and are often mixed up. '-**sure**' sounds like /**shur**/ or /**zure**/, while '-**ture**' sounds like /**chur**/.

A Complete each word using 'sure' or 'ture'.

mea	adven	trea	un
tempera	enclo	frac	pic
displea	carica	reas	imma

B Match each word to its meaning.

| sure | reassure | composure | mixture | culture | literature |

1. To make someone feel less afraid, upset or unsure
2. Written works such as plays, novels and poems
3. Something made by combining two or more ingredients
4. Without doubt
5. Calm
6. The beliefs, customs, etc. of a particular group or society

C Cross out the incorrect word in each sentence.

1. Before I leave in the morning, I ensure that I have my dentures lunchbox.
2. "May I have your signature gesture, please?" asked the delivery man.
3. It is with great sadness that we must announce the disclosure closure of the local park.
4. Barbara checked the departure fissure time for her flight three times before she went to bed.
5. The mountaineer is suffering from exposure architecture after his latest adventure.
6. "These exams are too much structure pressure!" cried Peter.

Grammar – Adjectives

An **adjective** is a word that describes a noun or pronoun. It usually comes before the noun (or pronoun), e.g. The **vicious** dog snapped at the **terrified** boy.

A Odd one out

Underline the adjective in each list that does not belong. Name the **simple** synonym that the remaining words describe. Use a dictionary or a thesaurus to help you.

1. feeble, scrawny, frail, brawny, fragile
2. gleeful, dismal, thrilled, ecstatic, contented
3. contemporary, decrepit, modern, recent, current
4. courteous, considerate, disrespectful, mannerly, gracious
5. arctic, chilly, frigid, freezing, sweltering

Adjectives can be organised into **seven groups** depending on what they describe about a noun. They are usually placed in the following order in a sentence:

1. Determiner (a word that shows the noun being described), e.g. this, the, a, some
2. Opinion, e.g. beautiful, terrifying, ugly, cruel, interesting, delightful
3. Size and shape, e.g. long, gigantic, minuscule, heavy, narrow, deep, square
4. Condition and age, e.g. ancient, tattered, wet, clean, pristine, modern
5. Colour and pattern, e.g. red, crimson, striped, checked, flowery, green, golden
6. Origin (nationality or religion), e.g. French, Muslim, Polish, Hindu, Irish
7. Material, e.g. wooden, silken, furry, diamond

B In your copy, rewrite these, placing the adjectives in the correct order and using commas to separate each list.

1. The striped old woollen ugly scarf fluttered in the wind.
2. Justin owns beautiful that stone modern big house.
3. My mum gave me this flowery pretty new dress.
4. I borrowed this French interesting tattered book from Gertrude.
5. Mrs Quinn is very proud of porcelain her antique patterned vase.
6. Andrea's dog is a scruffy huge terrifying mongrel, but she still loves him.

Top tip!

Usually, we use no more than three adjectives at a time.

C Dictation: Listen to your teacher and write the sentences in your copy.

 I can do this!   I'm getting there.   I need help!

Oral Language

A Five alive

In pairs, take it in turns to think of a place (e.g. the swimming pool, the schoolyard, a shopping centre) and describe it using your five senses. Your partner must guess the place you are describing using the clues that you give them.

Example:	I see …	I hear …	I smell …	I taste …	I feel …
The beach	people swimming.	waves crashing.	seaweed.	salt on my lips.	sand between my toes.

Points are given for each guess. The winner is the player with the **least** points.

Writing Genre – Narrative Writing

A **narrative** is a fictional story written to entertain the reader.

Structure:

- **Setting** – Introduce the setting, time and main character. Set the mood/tone.
- **Series of events** – This involves an initiating event (how the story starts) and a problem or conflict for the main character.
- **Resolution** – The problem is usually resolved for the main character.

A Plan, organise and write a narrative in which the main character/s go on a journey. Use the character's senses to describe the journey.

1. Complete a character profile for your main character using a mind map like the one below.

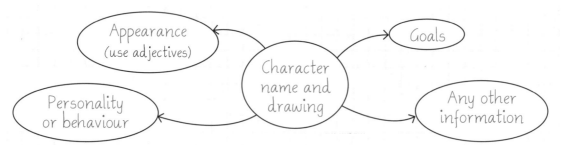

2. Complete this story plan.

Setting:	Who?	Where?	When?
Initiating event:			
Problem 1:			
Problem 2:			
Resolution:			

3. Use the character profile and story plan to write the first draft of your narrative.

B Debate: 'Bruno is a good friend to Shmuel.'

Siege

Comprehension Strategies

A Before reading: Character portrait

Use the strategy of **Visualising**. Without reading anything about him, draw a portrait of the character Captain Kelp in your copy. Record some key words you think might describe him. After reading, draw another portrait of him. Has your portrait changed? Why? Record some key words to describe his personality, thoughts and actions around the second portrait.

B Before reading: Changing predictions

Use the strategy of **Predicting**. In pairs, look at the title and illustration and predict what this text will be about – "I think this text will be about … because …"

Next, look at the key vocabulary below and make a new prediction based on this.

| crept | massive human | skulking | tactical position |
| squad | impressive | shields | cautious |

"My prediction has changed. Now, I think this text will be about … because …"

C During reading: Dictionary chart

Use the strategy of **Word Attack** and the skill of **Scanning**. Scan the text and write any interesting words in the chart below. Look for clues in the text to try to figure out the meaning. Finally, use a dictionary to find out if you were right.

Word	Meaning from the text	Was I right?

D After reading: Plot review

Use the strategy of **Synthesising**. As a class, list the main events of the text on flash cards. Next, hold the cards and line up in the order that the events happened.

Then, rate the event you are holding. Hold it up high if it was very exciting, hold it at your chest if it was normal and hold it low if it was not very exciting at all. Discuss and compare your reviews. This could be repeated with various different reactions to the text, e.g. sad, happy, interesting, etc.

Comprehension

STOP! Use your dictionary to find out the meaning of the **bold** words below.

Siege

Retrieval One crept together, making slightly less noise than a silk spider. Kelp did a quick head count. Eleven. One short of a full **compliment**. Four was probably **wandering** around the rose bushes, wondering why nobody was talking to him.

Then Trouble noticed two things – one, a pair of black boots was sticking out of a **shrub** beside the door, and two, there was a massive human standing in the doorway. The figure was **cradling** a very nasty-looking gun in the **crook** of his arm.

"Go silent," whispered Kelp, and **immediately** eleven full-face visors slid down to seal in the sounds of his squad's breathing and communications. [...]

The squad stepped back carefully until they were standing on the **manicured** grassy **verge**. The figure before them was indeed impressive, without doubt the biggest human any of them had ever seen.

"D'Arvit," breathed Two.

"**Maintain** radio silence, except in emergencies," ordered Kelp. "Swearing is hardly an emergency." Secretly however, he **concurred** with the **sentiment**. This was one time he was glad to be shielded. That man looked as if he could squash half a dozen fairies in one massive fist.

Grub returned to his slot. "Four is stable. **Concussed**, I'd guess. But otherwise OK. His shield's off though, so I stuffed him in the bushes."

"Well done, Corporal. Good thinking."

The last thing they needed was for Four's boots to be spotted.

The man moved, **lumbering casually** along the path. He may have **glanced** left or right, it was difficult to tell beneath the hood pulled over his eyes. Odd for a human to wear a hood on such a fine night [...]

The man mountain stopped, right in the middle of the squad. If he had been able to see them, it would be the perfect **tactical** position. Their own firearms were **virtually** useless, as they would probably do more damage to each other than the human.

Fortunately the entire squad was invisible, with the **exception** of Four, who was safely secreted in what **appeared** to be a **rhododendron**.

"Buzz batons. Fire 'em up."

Just in case. No harm being **cautious**.

And when the LEP officers were switching weapons, right at that moment when their hands were **fumbling** with **holsters**, that's when the Mud Man spoke.

"Evening gentlemen," he said, **sweeping** his hood back.

(From *'Artemis Fowl'* by Eoin Colfer)

A In your copy, go investigate.

1. What did Trouble notice standing in the doorway?

2. How many LEP officers make up a full compliment?

3. Who was checked on Four?

4. What is Kelp's nickname?

5. Where is Four now?

6. Why was it difficult to see the man's face?

B In your copy, give your opinion.

1. Why didn't the team hide when they saw the man?

2. Are these people human? What tells you this?

3. What do you think happened to Four?

4. Who do you think the leader of this team is? Why?

5. Did the retrieval team's shields work? How do you know?

6. What do you think will happen next?

C Vocabulary

1. Underline the part of each sentence that has been changed from the text.

   (a) The man moved, walking calmly along the path.

   (b) The figure was holding a very nasty-looking gun.

   (c) "Keep radio silence, except in emergencies."

   (d) Their own firearms were practically useless.

   (e) Straight away eleven full-face visors slid down.

   (f) No harm being careful.

   (g) A pair of black boots was sticking out of a bush beside the door.

2. In your copy, rewrite the sentences above in the order in which they occur in the text and insert the missing synonyms from the text.

D Cloze procedure: 'LEPretrieval One'. Fill in the blanks.

LEPretrieval _____ were the best _____ the brightest. It was every little fairy's _____ that one _____ he would grow _____ to don the stealth-black jumpsuit of the Retrieval commandos. These _____ the elite. Trouble was their _____ name. In the case of Captain Kelp, Trouble was actually _____ first _____. He'd insisted on it at _____ manhood ceremony, having just been accepted into the Academy.

Phonics – '-cial', '-tial'

'**-cial**' and '**-tial**' make a /**shul**/ sound. They are suffixes added to words to make an adjective, e.g. A president is elected from a presiden**tial** race.

'**-cial**' is usually used when the letter before it is a vowel, e.g. office → offi**cial**.

'**-tial**' is usually used when the letter before it is a consonant, e.g. residen**t** → residen**tial**.

A Match the root word to the correct '-cial' or '-tial' word.

1. glacier ▪   ▪ preferential
2. sequence ▪   ▪ judicial
3. society ▪   ▪ palatial
4. preference ▪   ▪ glacial
5. province ▪   ▪ sequential
6. palace ▪   ▪ social
7. space ▪   ▪ spatial
8. judge ▪   ▪ provincial

B Finish these words using either '-cial' or '-tial'. Then, write the root word. Use your dictionary to help you.

1. spe_____   species
2. par_____   _____
3. essen_____   _____
4. ra_____   _____
5. finan_____   _____
6. torren_____   _____
7. benefi_____   _____
8. influen_____   _____
9. substan_____   _____
10. fa_____   _____

C Ring the correct spelling in each sentence.

1. "I wish you would work to your full **potential / potencial**," said Matt's teacher.

2. My big sister is so **superfitial / superficial**, she won't leave the house without make-up.

3. I like **commercials / commertials** with catchy songs in them.

4. "This secret is **confidencial / confidential**. Don't tell anyone," whispered Ann.

5. Judges in competitions must be **impartial / imparcial** so there is no favouritism.

6. **Antisocial / Antisotial** behaviour can get you in trouble with the Gardaí.

7. The judge had **insubstancial / insubstantial** evidence to convict the criminal.

8. I don't like **artifitial / artificial** flowers, because they have no scent.

Grammar – Speech Marks

Speech marks (" ") are placed before and after **direct speech** to show exactly what a person has said. The punctuation (comma, full stop, exclamation mark or question mark) is always placed inside the speech marks.

Examples:　Helen asked Emma, "Can I borrow your pencil?"

"It's cold there," reported the meteorologist, "so wrap up warmly."

"I'm tired!" wailed the little boy.

A In your copy, rewrite these sentences using direct speech.

1. Mum told Jay to go upstairs and clean his room.

2. Irena asked Ethan to help her with her homework.

3. The lecturer told his students that their assignment was due next week.

4. The meteorologist announced that there would be a storm tomorrow.

5. Max asked where his glasses were. His mum said that they were upstairs.

6. Yasmina yelled at her sister to tidy up her side of the bedroom.

7. The marine biologist explained that a whale is actually a mammal.

When writing long pieces of **dialogue** in a story, begin a new paragraph each time the person speaking changes. This helps the reader to keep track of who is speaking.

Example:　"What are you doing inside, Tom?" asked Ms Martinez.

"I'm just looking for my jacket, Miss," explained Tom. "I can't find it."

B In your copy, rewrite this conversation using the correct punctuation.

Joanna get in here now shouted her mum. What is it asked Joanna as she ran into her bedroom. Your room looks like a bomb hit it replied Mum you need to clean it right now. Oh but Mum my favourite TV show is on, can I do it when it's over. I don't care Joanna, this is a disgrace. Ok fine sighed Joanna I'll watch TV later.

C In your copy, write the conversation between each pair.

1. An excited mother and daughter about to board an aeroplane

2. A girl looking guilty while a cross-looking man leans over her, pointing his finger at a broken window in the background

3. Two boys smiling widely, one is opening a birthday present from the other

4. A small boy crying, holding his cut knee, while an older child comforts him

D Dictation: Listen to your teacher and write the sentences in your copy.

I can do this! 　　I'm getting there. 　　I need help!

Oral Language

A My world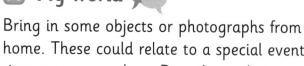

Bring in some objects or photographs from home. These could relate to a special event, time, person or place. Describe each item to the class, including memories and feelings. If you do not have an object of your own, use the pictures provided and create imaginary descriptions, memories and feelings.

Writing Genre – Narrative Writing

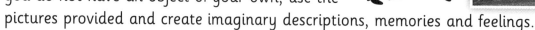

The **language of a narrative** should include:

- nouns and pronouns that refer to specific characters, e.g. they, he, Bruno.
- first or third person: I, we or he, they, she.
- past tense, e.g. roamed, exclaimed.
- action verbs, e.g. crept, fluttered.
- descriptive adjectives used to create imagery, e.g. sluggish, mystical, hideous.
- linking words to show time, e.g. early the next morning, at the same time.
- dialogue using direct speech, e.g. "What do you think you're doing?" shouted the Garda.
- verbs showing what was said, thought or felt, e.g. announced, wondered, snapped.
- language devices to create imagery, e.g. similes, metaphors, onomatopoeia.

A Review, edit and rewrite your journey narrative.

1. Make sure that your narrative has all of the following:
   - Setting
   - Series of events – an initiating event and two problems
   - Resolution
   - Narrative language

2. Read over your narrative and edit it for spelling, punctuation and grammar.

3. Rewrite your narrative and include:
   - An illustration
   - An interesting title

4. Check your work using the narrative self-assessment checklist.

B Art activity

Draw the journey your character takes on a scroll of paper. Add a short description or a piece of dialogue to each illustration.

Greg got a compass for his birthday, which he used to go exploring.

Along the way, he battled lions and saved his sister from crocodile-infested rivers.

He returned home a hero.

Hope Is the Thing with Feathers

Comprehension Strategies

A Before reading: Changing images

Use the strategy of **Visualising**. Draw a picture to show what you can picture …

Before reading	During reading	After reading

B During reading

Use the strategy of **Clarifying**. We need something clarified when we read a word, a phrase or an idea that we don't understand. Here are some steps to help you clarify:

- Read back.
- Read on.
- Think of your schema. Do you have any background knowledge that might help?
- Is there any information in the image/s that might help?
- Might another phrase make sense here?

C During reading: I think that … because …

Use the strategy of **Inferring**. As you read, stop along the way to make inferences with evidence from the text.

- Reading between the lines, I think that … because …
- The poet says … but I think she means … because …
- I think the poet feels … because …

D After reading: Deciphering poetry

Use the strategy of **Synthesising**. In pairs, talk about each stanza (verse). Can you explain what the poet means in each line? Together, write a single line to explain each stanza.

Comprehension

 Use your dictionary to find out the meaning of the **bold** words below.

Hope Is the Thing with Feathers

Hope is the thing with feathers
That **perches** in the soul,
And sings the tune without the words,
And never stops at all,

And sweetest in the **gale** is heard;
And sore must be the storm
That could **abash** the little bird
That kept so many warm.

I've heard it in the chillest land,
And on the strangest sea,
Yet, never, in **extremity**,
It asked a crumb of me.

By Emily Dickinson

A In your copy, go investigate.

1. To what animal is the poet comparing hope?

2. Where does the bird perch? Why do you think it perches there?

3. How does the bird convey its message of hope?

4. What kind of song does the bird sing?

5. What does the poet say could 'abash the little bird'?

6. Where has the author 'heard' the bird?

B In your copy, give your opinion.

1. Do you think this is a good metaphor? Why?

2. Can you think of another animal you would compare hope to?

3. Why do you think the poet says 'and never stops at all' in stanza one?

4. What does the poet mean by 'that kept so many warm' in stanza two?

5. Do you like this poem? Why/Why not?

6. Draw a picture of a bird that represents hope to you.

Top tip!

A metaphor describes something by comparing it to something else.

C Vocabulary

1. Write a list of vocabulary that you would associate with birds. Use nouns, verbs, adjectives and adverbs.

feathers		
flap		
graceful		

2. The rhyming words in this poem aren't always obvious, e.g. 'words', 'heard' and 'bird'. In your copy, find pairs or groups of rhyming words in the poem and add your own words to the list, e.g. 'words', 'heard', 'bird', 'shared', 'paired'.

D Cloze procedure: 'Emily Dickinson'. Fill in the blanks.

Emily _____ was an American poet. She was _____ in Massachusetts in 1830 and lived there all her _____. Her father was a lawyer and her mother was a quiet _____. Emily had a younger sister, Lavinia, and an _____ brother, Austin. Emily _____ also a quiet woman and didn't have _____ friends. Altogether, she _____ nearly 1,800 poems, but less than a dozen of these were published while she was _____. Although she was unpopular during her lifetime for breaking the conventional rules of poetry, she is now considered to be _____ of the greatest American _____.

Phonics – Rhyming Words

Rhyme occurs when the endings of words sound similar, but rhyming words do not necessarily have the same spelling, e.g. 'here' and 'fear', 'chair' and 'hare'.

A Match each word to a rhyming word.

1. pie ▪
2. school ▪
3. tissue ▪
4. monkey ▪
5. phone ▪
6. photo ▪
7. keyboard ▪

▪ groan
▪ buy
▪ toward
▪ chew
▪ blow
▪ chunky
▪ rule

B Write the rhyming words for each pair of clues.

1. A small river	_____ _____	1. Similar to milk, but thicker
2. A utensil for cutting	_____ _____	2. Opposite of husband
3. Found on a tree	_____ _____	3. A person who steals
4. Hope or want	_____ _____	4. A creature that lives in water
5. Worn on the finger	_____ _____	5. Male ruler of a country
6. Keeps food cool	_____ _____	6. A path or road over a river
7. Grows on the head	_____ _____	7. A four-sided shape
8. A stinging plant	_____ _____	8. A colourful part of a flower

C In your copy, rewrite these sentences. Replace the words that don't belong with a rhyming word that does.

write   food   our   hate   teacher   cold   floor   friend

1. Samantha is excited to go to the same secondary school as her blend.
2. "Don't throw your clothes on the boar, Seamus!" cried his mum.
3. We are not allowed to light in pen without a pen licence in our class.
4. My favourite dude is strawberry ice-cream.
5. Venus is the hottest planet in flower Solar System.
6. Winter in Ireland is very mould and wet.
7. Our creature is an excellent singer. I love it when he teaches us songs.
8. "Change the channel, Barry. I eight this programme," complained Lisa.

Grammar – Similes and Metaphors

A **simile** is a figure of speech that compares two things using the words 'like' or 'as', e.g. as black as coal, she looks like death warmed up.

A Match each simile to the correct ending.

1. As easy as ■	■ whistle.	5. As bold as ■	■ log.
2. Life is like a ■	■ pie.	6. I slept like a ■	■ cucumber.
3. As clean as a ■	■ glove.	7. As cool as a ■	■ ghost.
4. It fits like a ■	■ box of chocolates.	8. As white as a ■	■ brass.

A **metaphor** is also a figure of speech that compare two things, but **without** using the words 'like' or 'as'. It also helps an author to describe something and often doesn't make sense if you listen to the literal (exact) meaning, e.g. time is money.

B Complete each metaphor using the correct word.

1. Don't judge a book by its _____. (author, cover, characters)

2. It's raining cats and _____ out there. (dogs, mice, snow)

3. Time _____ by when you are having fun. (walks, flies, runs)

4. Your lovely voice is like _____ to my ears. (wind, words, music)

5. Debbie called Libby a _____, because she was scared. (mouse, cat, chicken)

6. My teacher says that I have a heart of _____. (copper, gold, silver)

C Finish each sentence and tick for simile (S) or metaphor (M).

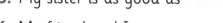

a rug   feet   blanket   a log   in a pod   gold   paint dry

	S	M
1. The play was so boring, it was like watching _____.		
2. The man didn't get married, because he got cold _____.		
3. I am as snug as a bug in _____ in my new pyjamas.		
4. When I woke up, there was a _____ of snow on the ground.		
5. My sister is as good as _____ in school.		
6. My friend and I are two peas _____.		
7. I was so tired yesterday, I slept like _____.		

D Dictation: Listen to your teacher and write the sentences in your copy.

 I can do this!   I'm getting there.   I need help!

Oral Language

A Something different

In pairs, pick any ordinary object. Give yourselves two minutes to write down as many different ways to describe it as possible. When the time is up, compare your answers and cross off any that are the same. The person with the most answers left wins.

Example: A tree

- A shelter-provider
- A life-giver
- A home
- Rainbow foliage
- A source of fuel

Writing Genre – Poetry Writing

Do you remember that a **poem** is a fictional piece of writing that entertains the reader? Poetry has many different language features, including:

- nouns and verbs that refer to specific objects, events, emotions, things or actions.
- adjectives and adverbs that are more imaginative than factual, e.g. weary, ecstatic.
- literary devices such as rhyme, rhythm, imagery, alliteration, assonance, repetition, onomatopoeia, simile, metaphor and symbolism.

A Write a poem using an animal as a metaphor for a feeling.

1. Plan your poem.
   - Think of an emotion or feeling that you would like to write about.
   - Think of an animal that might be a good metaphor for this feeling.
   - Brainstorm some actions, words or symbols that are associated with this animal that might help you to portray your metaphor, e.g.

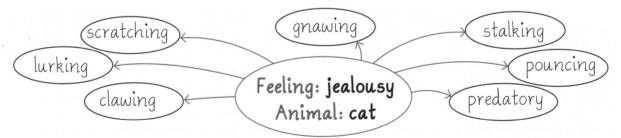

2. Use the pattern of 'Hope Is the Thing with Feathers' to guide your poem, i.e. three stanzas of four lines each with an ABCB, ABAB, ABBB rhyming pattern.

3. Write your poem using a title similar to the original, e.g. 'Jealousy Is the Thing with Whiskers'.

B Art activity

Think of the emotion that your metaphor represents and imagine a colour associated with it, e.g. green for jealously. Use that colour of paint, blended with a little white or black to create light or shade, to paint a picture of your chosen animal. Wait for the paint to dry fully and then write your poem over the painting.

How Does a Thermometer Work?

Comprehension Strategies

A Before reading: KWL chart

Use the strategies of **Making Connections** and **Questioning**. In your copy, draw a chart like the one below. Then, glance at the headings in the text and complete your chart.

KWL Chart			
What I know	**What I want to know**	**What I have learned**	**Keywords to use in an internet search about thermometers**

B During reading: Fabulous five

Use the strategy of **Determining Importance**. While reading, record five key words in the text. Then, in groups, compare your 'fabulous five' and justify why you thought these were the most important words in the text.

C After reading: 3, 2, 1

Use the strategy of **Synthesising**.

Three things that I learned from the text:

▪ _____

▪ _____

▪ _____

Two interesting facts in the text:

▪ _____

▪ _____

One question that I still have:

▪ _____

Comprehension

STOP! Use your dictionary to find out the meaning of the **bold** words below.

How Does a Thermometer Work?

A **thermometer** is a **device** used to measure **temperature**.

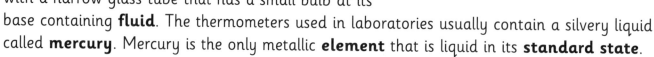

Mercury | Glass tube | Bulb | Temperature markings

How does it work?

The bulb thermometer is the most widely known type of thermometer. It is made with a narrow glass tube that has a small bulb at its base containing **fluid**. The thermometers used in laboratories usually contain a silvery liquid called **mercury**. Mercury is the only metallic **element** that is liquid in its **standard state**.

The **volume** of a liquid changes **depending** on its temperature. Cold temperatures cause it to take up less space and warm temperatures mean it takes up more space. All liquids share this **property**. Mercury is used in thermometers because it has a higher boiling point and a lower freezing point than most other liquids. This means that it needs to be very hot before it will boil and very cold before it will freeze. However, mercury is **toxic** when it comes into **contact** with the skin. As a result, alcohol or galinstan (another liquid element) have become more widely used in bulb thermometers. Both also have a high boiling point and a low freezing point.

As the thermometer's bulb is small, the liquid inside it quickly reaches the temperature of the **substance** being measured. The liquid then **expands** or **contracts** depending on how hot or cold the substance is. We can then look at the markings on the side of the thermometer to gain an **accurate** reading of the temperature.

Most people now use digital thermometers, which are are safer and easier to read, and work faster.

How do we measure temperature?

There are two different units of measurement for temperature: Fahrenheit and Celsius. In Ireland, we use the Celsius **scale** (°C). Celsius measures the freezing point of water as 0°C and the boiling point of water as 100°C. We **define** room temperature as the temperature at which a room feels neither warm nor cold when wearing typical indoor clothing. This scale ranges from 15°C to 25°C. Normal body temperature is defined as 36.5°C to 37.5°C.

What are thermometers used for?

Thermometers have many uses. They are used to **determine** road temperatures in order to **predict** freezing, to measure **optimum** temperatures for cooking, to record body temperatures in medicine and to **forecast** the weather.

Thermometers have many different uses in our everyday lives. They are important in cooking, in health and in scientific experiments. Reading a bulb thermometer is an important skill. However, this is becoming less popular due to safety **concerns**.

A In your copy, go investigate.

1. What materials is a bulb thermometer made with?
2. Describe what mercury looks like in its typical state.
3. Why are liquids used to measure temperature?
4. What other thermometers are now used instead of mercury thermometers?
5. Why are these other thermometers used?
6. What does 'room temperature' mean?

Mercury

B In your copy, give your opinion.

1. Explain in your own words how a bulb thermometer works.
2. Would a thermometer made with very thick glass work well? Why/Why not?
3. What special property makes mercury the best liquid for use in a thermometer?
4. Why is this special property useful to accurately measure the temperature?
5. What might it mean if your body temperature is higher than 37.5°C?
6. What do you think is the most important use of a thermometer?

C Vocabulary: Match each word from the text to its meaning.

| scale | volume | expand | optimum | accurate | define | property |

1. An important quality or characteristic of a thing
2. A series of equal steps or marks used for measurement
3. The best or most favourable circumstance
4. To describe, explain or identify the properties of
5. To increase in size
6. Without error or mistake
7. The amount of space an object or substance occupies

D Cloze procedure: 'Fahrenheit and Celsius'. Fill in the blanks.

The earliest thermometer was known as a thermoscope. It could only _____ if something was getting hotter or _____ and could not measure the temperature. Daniel Gabriel Fahrenheit invented the _____ thermometer with a standard scale. He first _____ alcohol in 1709 and later used mercury _____ 1714. He introduced the Fahrenheit scale in 1724. This was the first time that changes in _____ could be measured accurately. In 1742, the Swedish astronomer Anders Celsius introduced the simpler _____ scale of 100 degrees between the freezing _____ (0°C) and the boiling point (100 ___) of water. This scale is used in many areas of the _____ today.

Phonics – '-ate'

'**-ate**' is a suffix added to nouns or adjectives to make verbs, e.g.
to vaccin**ate** (give someone a vaccination) or to frustr**ate** (cause frustration).

A Change each word to a verb using '-ate'. Some words will need to have letters removed or added before adding the suffix.

1. assassin
2. participant
3. formula
4. hibernation
5. captive
6. fascination
7. pollen
8. confiscation
9. origin
10. nomination
11. active
12. complication
13. valid
14. decor
15. hydration
16. refrigerator

B Complete the crossword using '-ate' words.

Across

3. To keep apart (s)
5. To add artwork, usually to books (i)
6. To turn or revolve (r)
8. To make complex or difficult (c)
9. To find (l)
10. To annoy or irritate (f)

Down

1. To work together (c)
2. To embarrass (h)
4. To destroy completely (e)
7. To be grateful or thankful for (a)

C In your copy, write a sentence using each of the '-ate' words above.

Grammar – Prepositions

A **preposition** relates a noun or a pronoun to another word. It often refers to where or when something is happening. 'Pre' means before and 'position' means place, so preposition means 'placed before'. For a word to be a preposition, it must be placed before the noun.

Examples: I went to the cinema **with** my friends.

We must wear our uniform **during** school.

A Complete each sentence using an appropriate preposition. Tick whether the preposition refers to where or when.

	Where	When
1. Piper threw her bag _____ the couch when she got home.		
2. My sister hid _____ the curtains during hide-and-seek.		
3. Our class works hard _____ the day.		
4. Conor stood _____ a man in the queue.		
5. Matty slept _____ midday when he was sick.		
6. My big brother cut the grass _____ I washed the windows.		
7. My neighbour's dog often tries to jump _____ the fence.		
8. We get dessert _____ dinner on Sundays.		
9. Niamh found her lost bag _____ her bed.		

A **preposition** can be used together with a noun to make a preposistional phrase, e.g. **around** the bend, **under** the stairs.

B Match each preposition to the correct noun to create a prepositional phrase. In your copy, write a sentence for each.

1. without ▪	▪ the house	7. on ▪	▪ you and me
2. opposite ▪	▪ the winter	8. between ▪	▪ time
3. during ▪	▪ Christmas	9. under ▪	▪ the river
4. for ▪	▪ the world	10. along ▪	▪ arrest
5. by ▪	▪ the ocean	11. through ▪	▪ my friends
6. around ▪	▪ delay	12. next to ▪	▪ the forest

C Dictation: Listen to your teacher and write the sentences in your copy.

 I can do this!   I'm getting there.   I need help!

Oral Language

A Alien invasion

Imagine that you are an alien. Choose one of the objects pictured below (or another simple object) and explain how you think it works. The most inventive explanation wins.

> This is clearly a powerful weapon. When this button is pressed, dust particles from the air are sucked into the vents on the side. The dust particles are compressed and the newly formed bullets are propelled with a gust of air out of the nozzle at the front.

Example:
a hairdryer

Writing Genre – Explanation Writing

An **explanation** is a text that explains how something works, or how or why something happens.

Structure:

- **Title** – Usually presented in the form of a question.
- **Definition** – A brief description or fact about the thing you will be explaining.
- **Description** – A logical, step-by-step explanation of how or reasons why, often supported by diagrams.
- **Applications** – What the object is designed to do or can be used for.
- **Summary** – A brief summary of the main points.

Top tip!

Explanations are not 'how to' texts. Those are instructions.

A Design a simple new invention. Plan, organise and write an explanation of how your invention works.

1. In your copy, plan your explanation using a framework like the one below.

1. **Invention:**	2. **Title:** How a _____ works.
3. **Definition** (brief description or fact about the invention)	4. **Description** (detailed steps on how it works, including cause and effect)
5. **Applications** (when and where to use it)	6. **Summary**

2. Use your plan to write the first draft of your explanation.

B Debate: 'All mercury thermometers should be banned.'

How Does a Plant Make Food?

Comprehension Strategies

A Before reading: Think sheet

Use the strategies of **Predicting** and **Questioning**. Below are the headings found in the text.

- What does a plant need to make food?
- What happens in the process of photosynthesis?
- What does photosynthesis mean for us?
- What does photosynthesis mean?

In pairs, complete the following in your copy:

- Our predictions for the answers to the questions above
- What the text actually says (Complete this after reading.)

B During reading: Stop and think

Use the strategy of **Questioning**. As you read each section, stop to think:

- Did I understand this section?
- Were there any parts that I didn't understand?
- Could I explain this information to someone else?
- Are there any questions that I need to have answered?

C During reading: Turn on the lights!

Use the strategy of **Clarifying**. Stop and notice when you have a a 'lightbulb moment'. This is when something in the text is clarified or explained. Record your lightbulb moments below.

D After reading: Main-idea sort

Use the strategies of **Determining Importance** and **Summarising**. In groups, record the main ideas, phrases and keywords on flash cards. Arrange the main ideas, phrases and keywords under the headings from the text. Without looking back through the text, use these to create a summary of the text. Share your summary with the class.

Comprehension

STOP! Use your dictionary to find out the meaning of the **bold** words below.

How Does a Plant Make Food?

The answer… photosynthesis! Humans and animals get the energy to learn, run and do everyday tasks from the food that we eat. Plants don't take in food in the way that we do. They make their own through a **process** called photosynthesis.

What does a plant need to make food?

- **Carbon dioxide** in the air is absorbed through **pores** in the leaves called stoma.
- **Water** is absorbed through the roots and travels through **vessels** in the stem to the leaves.
- **Sunlight** (light energy) is absorbed by a green **chemical** in the leaves' **cells** called chlorophyll.

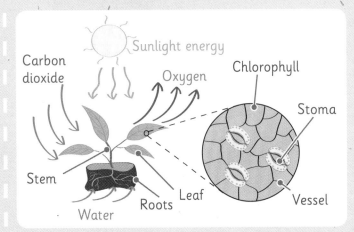

What happens in the process of photosynthesis?

1. Chlorophyll absorbs the sun's energy.
2. This energy splits water (H_2O) **molecules** into hydrogen (H) and oxygen (O).
3. The leaves **release** oxygen into the **atmosphere**.
4. Hydrogen and carbon dioxide **combine** to make glucose or sugar.
5. Some of the glucose is used as food energy to help the plant to grow. The rest is **stored** in leaves, fruit or roots for later use.

What does photosynthesis mean for us?

- The glucose that plants store is the energy that humans and animals absorb when they eat vegetables and fruit. Even when we eat meat, we get plant energy.
- Plants release oxygen, which we need to breathe. We couldn't exist without photosynthesis!
- When humans breathe, we breathe out carbon dioxide. This chemical is **harmful** to the environment. Plants help to balance the oxygen and carbon dioxide levels in the atmosphere.
- Most of the energy that we use to heat our homes or power our cars comes from **fossil fuels** such as natural gas, oil and coal. These fossil fuels are the **remains** of dead plants and animals stored in the earth for millions of years. They got their energy from photosynthesis. Burning these fuels releases carbon dioxide, which plants absorb.

What does photosynthesis mean?

'Photo' is a Greek word meaning 'light'. 'Synthesis' is a Greek word meaning 'putting together'.

Imagine being able to eat without going to the shop or even touching a saucepan. Well this is exactly what plants do in the **fascinating** process of photosynthesis. However, photosynthesis does much more than **provide** food for plants. It provides food, energy and clean air for humans too.

A In your copy, go investigate.

1. What three things does a plant need for photosynthesis?

2. How does a plant take in carbon dioxide?

3. What does a plant produce in the process of photosynthesis?

4. Name the food energy that helps plants to grow.

5. Where do people get most of the energy to fuel our cars and homes?

6. Is this a good thing? Why/Why not?

B In your copy, give your opinion.

1. Why do you think plants store glucose instead of using it all up straight away?

2. Does the term 'photosynthesis' describe the process well? Why/Why not?

3. What do you think gives plants their green colour?

4. Would you prefer to get your energy through photosynthesis? Why/Why not?

5. Has learning about photosynthesis made you want to plant trees? Why?

6. What do you think is the most interesting or surprising part of photosynthesis?

C Vocabulary: cause and effect

Cause and effect is when one event causes another to happen. Tick the box that accurately describes the effects of each cause mentioned in the text.

Cause	Effect	
1. Humans breathe out carbon dioxide.	▪ Plants absorb the carbon dioxide.	
	▪ The sun absorbs the carbon dioxide.	
2. Leaves release oxygen.	▪ The oxygen harms the environment.	
	▪ Humans and animals breathe in oxygen.	
3. Hydrogen and carbon dioxide combine.	▪ Glucose is formed.	
	▪ Humans and animals make food with this.	

D Cloze procedure: 'Energy'. Fill in the blanks.

Millions of _____ ago, plants absorbed the sun's energy through _____.
Animals ate the plants, absorbing _____. When the _____ and animals died,
they became buried and compressed in the earth. Humans now harness this energy in the form
of oil, natural gas and _____, all of which we call fossil fuels. Burning fossil _____
releases harmful gasses such as carbon _____ into the atmosphere. Not only are
fossil fuels bad for the _____, they are also non-renewable, meaning they can
only be used once. _____ sources of energy such as solar, hydro or wind energy
can be used over and over and are not _____ to the environment.

Phonics – Heteronyms

Homographs (coming from the Latin words 'homos', 'same', and 'graphos', 'writing') are words that are spelled the same and may sound the same, but have different meanings.
Heteronyms are spelled the same, but <u>sound different</u> and have different meanings.
e.g. close – near to, to shut.

A Write the word described by each pair of pictures. In pairs, say each word aloud to remember the different pronunciation.

B Write the correct heteronym.

1. Drop of salty fluid that is the result of crying
   To rip paper or material

2. One-sixtieth of an hour
   Extremely small in size

3. Flesh injury
   Past tense of 'wind'

4. In the current moment
   To give or offer a gift or important item

5. To look at something written for understanding
   The past tense of the word above

6. To continue to exist
   Happening right now, not recorded or taped

C In your copy, write a sentence to show the two meanings of each heteronym below.

The meaning of these words changes depending on which syllable the stress is placed on, e.g. **in**valid/in**val**id.

1. console, 2. permit, 3. suspect, 4. content, 5. object, 6. record

Grammar – Pronouns

A **pronoun** is a word that takes the place of one or more nouns.

Personal pronouns replace people or things (he, it, them),
e.g. **Sarah** goes to ballet class with **Fiona** and **Oliver**.
→ **She** goes to ballet class with **them**.

A **possessive pronoun** shows ownership (mine, theirs).
It is placed after or instead of the noun, e.g. I know that's **my** coat. → That's **mine**.

> **Remember!**
>
> Possessive pronouns **replace** or come **after** the noun, e.g. That car is **his**.
>
> Possessive adjectives describe the noun, e.g That is **his** car.

A In your copy, replace the underlined words in these sentences with the correct pronoun.

1. <u>Joseph and Grace</u> love to go <u>to the park</u> together," said <u>Joseph and Grace</u>.

2. These are <u>my glasses</u>. Where are <u>your glasses</u>?

3. <u>The man</u> wears his suit to work every day.

4. "That is <u>our toy</u>," said Amelia and Miranda.

5. <u>Richard</u> gave <u>his dog</u> to <u>the vet</u>.

6. "I did <u>Izzy's</u> homework. Did <u>Alex</u> do <u>Alex's</u> homework?" said Izzy to Alex.

A **relative pronoun** connects clauses or phrases that provide additional information to the rest of the sentence, e.g. The man **who** stole the money went to prison.

a clause

- Who – the person performing the action
- Whose – the possessive form of 'who'
- Which – objects and non-essential information
- That – people or objects and essential information
- Whom – the person whom the action is being done to/for/about

> **Top tip!**
>
> Non-essential clauses are separated from the rest of the sentence with commas.

B Use the correct relative pronoun to complete each sentence.

1. The man   wallet this is must be looking for it.

2. The doctor   saved my life is my hero.

3. I really enjoyed the book   our teacher told us to read.

4. Mount Everest,   is the tallest mountain in the world, is in Nepal.

5. The girl   I walk to school with is every day is my good friend.

C Dictation: Listen to your teacher and write the sentences in your copy.

 I can do this!   I'm getting there.   I need help!

Oral Language

A Cause and effect

In pairs, explain the cause and effect of what has happened in these pictures. Next, draw a picture for your partner and have them explain the cause and effect.

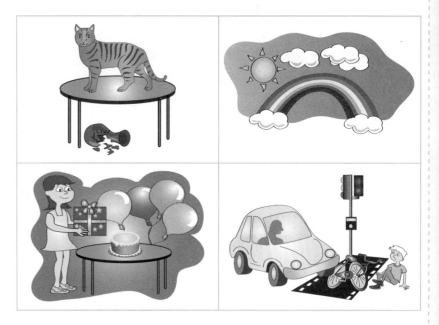

Writing Genre – Explanation Writing

The **language of an explanation** should include:

- general, non-human subjects, e.g. the plant, the volcanoes, the lungs.
- time conjunctions, e.g. eventually, before this happens.
- cause and effect conjunctions, e.g. consequently, the reason that.
- mostly action verbs, e.g. forms, transforms.
- timeless present tense verbs, e.g. happens, soaks.
- clear and factual adjectives, e.g. condensed, renewable.
- technical terms, e.g. condensation, tectonic plates, chlorophyll.
- formal, objective style, i.e. first-person pronouns and the writer's opinion are not used.

A Review, edit and rewrite your explanation in the form of a leaflet.

1. Make sure that your explanation has all of the following:
   - Title
   - Definition
   - Description
   - Applications
   - Summary
   - Explanation language

2. Read over your explanation and edit it for spelling, punctuation and grammar.

3. Rewrite your explanation as a leaflet and include each step of the sequence.

4. Check your work using the explanation self-assessment checklist.

B Art activity

Use various recycled materials (e.g. cereal boxes, toilet roll tubes, paper cups, bottle lids, straws and scraps of coloured paper) to construct your new invention.

Display your invention along with the leaflet for your classmates to investigate.

Luta de Galo

Comprehension Strategies

A Before reading: How to play

Use the strategy of **Predicting**. Read the title of the text and look at the picture. Use your crystal ball to predict the steps of how to play the game.

> I predict that…

> I imagine that…

> I wonder if…

> I think that…

> I think that… will happen, because…

> Maybe… will happen, because…

B During reading: Fabulous five

Use the strategy of **Determining Importance**. While reading, record five key words in the text. Then, in groups, compare your 'fabulous five' and justify why you thought these were the most important words in the text.

C After reading: Shared retells

Use the strategy of **Summarising** and the skill of **Skimming**. In pairs, take turns naming the steps of the game without looking at the text:

- Pupil A – step one
- Pupil B – step two … and so on.

When you have finished, skim the text to make sure that you didn't leave anything out. Keep going until you are able to explain the game without leaving out any steps.

D After reading: Informative images

Use the strategy of **Visualising**. In groups, work together to create one or two images that will accurately describe how to play the game without needing to read the text. Draw the image/s as a poster and have a competition to decide which poster will be displayed in the yard to show other classes how to play the game.

Comprehension

 STOP! Use your dictionary to find out the meaning of the **bold** words below.

Luta de Galo

Aim: To learn how to play the game *Luta de Galo*.

Equipment:

- A handkerchief, napkin or other piece of cloth for each child

Children play in pairs.

This is a **traditional** children's game from Brazil. *Luta de Galo* is Portuguese for 'fight of the roosters'.

Diagram:

Dominant arm crossed over chest

Handkerchief

One leg raised

Method:

1. Tuck the handkerchief into the waistband of your trousers with enough sticking out so that your **opponent** can grab it.

2. Cross your **dominant** hand over your chest, as you are not **permitted** to use this hand during the game.

3. Lift one foot, so that you are hopping on one leg.

4. Each player must then **attempt** to steal the handkerchief belonging to the other person, while protecting their own handkerchief at the same time.

5. The first player to capture their opponent's handkerchief is the winner.

6. If any player uncrosses their dominant arm or touches the ground with their lifted foot, they are **disqualified**.

Variations:

Luta de Galo can be played with more than two players. The winner would be the last child left with their handkerchief still in place.

You might like to play this game blindfolded to make it even harder. Be sure to play on a soft **surface** such as grass if you decide to try this.

This game could also be played in teams, with each team having their own colour of handkerchief. Each team should have a supply of handkerchiefs so that a player can keep playing once their handkerchief has been taken, by tucking a new one into their waistband. The aim is to catch as many handkerchiefs belonging to other teams as possible before the time runs out or your team has no handkerchiefs left.

A In your copy, go investigate.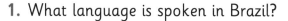

1. What language is spoken in Brazil?

2. What equipment is needed for this game?

3. What is the aim of this game?

4. Which arm should *you* cross over your chest when playing *Luta de Galo*?

5. In what ways might a player lose when playing *Luta de Galo*?

6. Would this be an easy game to organise? Why/Why not?

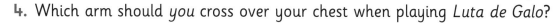

The Brazilian flag

B In your copy, give your opinion.

1. Why do you think this game is called 'fight of the roosters'?

2. Can you think of another name that would be suitable for this game?

3. Why do you think the players cross their dominant arm over their chest and hop on one foot while playing *Luta de Galo*?

4. Why would you need to play on a soft surface if you were to play the game blindfolded?

5. Can you think of any other rules that would make this game more interesting?

6. Would you like to play *Luta de Galo*? Why/Why not?

C Vocabulary: Underline the odd one out in each list of synonyms below and ring the word from the text.

1. while, during, amidst, separate, throughout

2. rival, challenger, ally, opponent, adversary

3. permitted, allowed, authorised, prohibited, sanctioned

4. release, seize, capture, arrest, abduct

5. classic, modern, historic, traditional, time-honoured

6. try, attempt, endeavour, bid, retreat

D Cloze procedure: 'Duck, Duck, Goose'. Fill in the blanks.

'Duck, Duck, Goose' is a playground game played with many variations by children around the

_____. There is no _____ needed for this game. A group of children

sit together in a circle. The child _____ is 'it' walks around the outside of the circle, gently

_____ the others on the head, saying "duck" each _____. When 'it' taps someone

on the head and says "_____", that person must stand up and chase 'it' around _____

circle. 'It' must try to run around the _____ circle and steal the spot of the person whom

they have just chosen. If 'it' gets _____ before they sit down, they remain on. If they

are not caught, the new person is now 'it' and the _____ continues.

Phonics – 'y'

'**y**' has many different sounds.
- '**y**' can make a /**yuh**/ sound, e.g. **y**es.
- '**y**' can make an /**ee**/ sound, e.g. happ**y**.
- '**y**' can make a long /**i**/ sound, e.g. m**y**.
- '**y**' can make a short /**i**/ sound, e.g. bic**y**cle.

A In your copy, draw a table like the one below. Sort these 'y' words into the correct boxes. Add at least two of your own to each box.

mystery	yacht	butterfly	crystal	yellow
mystify	activity	oxygen	battery	syrup
ancestry	yawn	qualify	magnify	pharmacy

/yuh/	/ee/	Long /i/	Short /i/

B Match each word to its meaning.

1. The yellow part of an egg ▪
2. A young swan ▪
3. To exchange money for goods or services ▪
4. A boat used for leisure activities ▪
5. A religious song ▪
6. A small, red, acidic berry ▪
7. To make easier ▪
8. An amount of something ▪

▪ buy
▪ cranberry
▪ yacht
▪ quantity
▪ simplify
▪ cygnet
▪ yolk
▪ hymn

C Complete each sentence using the correct 'y' word. Write the correct 'y' sound beside each sentence.

| pigsty | surgery | myths | yoghurt | mummifying | Egyptians | every | syrup |

1. Arthur has a strawberry _____ for his lunch _____ day. <u>yuh and ee</u>

2. "Tidy your room. It looks like a _____!" shouted Tim's mum. _____

3. Nia loves to pour maple _____ on her pancakes. _____

4. Ireland has many famous _____ and legends. _____

5. "I'm afraid your knee will need _____," announced the doctor. _____

6. The Ancient _____ were famous for _____ their dead. _____

Grammar – Adverbs

An **adverb** is a word that describes a verb. It usually (but not always) ends in '**-ly**'. **Adverbs** tell us how (**manner**), where (**place**), when (**time**), how much (**degree**) or how often (**frequency**) something happens.

Examples: Charlie walked **carefully** across the road. (**manner**)

Mark ran **away**. (**place**)

She painted **yesterday**. (**time**)

Mishaal is **almost** finished her book. (**degree**)

Theo **always** has sandwiches for lunch. (**frequency**)

> **Top tip!**
>
> It helps to ask **how**, **where**, **when**, **how much** or **how often** if you are unsure of the adverb in a sentence.

A Underline the verbs. Ring the adverbs that describe them in these sentences and classify them in the table below.

1. Vladimir barely feels the cold in Ireland, because he used to live in Russia.

2. "Can we eat there?" asked Gillian, pointing to a pizza restaurant.

3. The ballerina danced gracefully across the stage.

4. My class has a weekly spellings test.

5. I am going to the cinema tomorrow.

6. Filip went abroad over the summer holidays.

7. Reem occasionally rides her bike to school.

8. "Have you eaten enough?" asked Ian.

9. "He deliberately ruined my project to make his look better!" cried Angela.

10. "Did you have a chance to fix my car yet?" Mariam asked the mechanic.

Manner (how)	Place (where)	Time (when)	Degree (how much)	Frequency (how often)

B In your copy, write a sentence for each adverb below. After each sentence, write in brackets which type of adverb is used.

1. completely 2. sometimes 3. upstairs 4. hurriedly 5. often

6. here 7. furiously 8. already 9. eventually 10. nearly

C Dictation: Listen to your teacher and write the sentences in your copy.

 I can do this!   I'm getting there.   I need help!

Oral Language

A Game makers

Work with a partner to create a new game using a random collection of PE equipment provided by your teacher. Think about:

- Is this an individual or a team game?
- How many people are on a team?
- What age group will be playing?
- What are the rules?
- How are points scored?
- How is the game won?

Present your game to the class.

Writing Genre – Procedural Writing

A **procedure** is a text that explains how something is done through a series of steps.

Structure:

- **Aim** – Explains what's to be done; often found in the title, e.g. How to use the oven.
- **Materials or equipment** – A list of what's needed, e.g. ingredients, tools, parts, etc.
- **Method** – A series of sequential steps, usually organised in bullet point form. Sub-headings, diagrams or photographs may be included.
- **Conclusion or evaluation** – States how success can be measured. Some procedures include variations of this e.g. Enjoy the game!, other ideas, etc.

A Plan, organise and write instructions for how to play a new game.

Tip: You could use the game created in the oral language activity above.

1. In your copy, plan your game using a mind map like the one below.

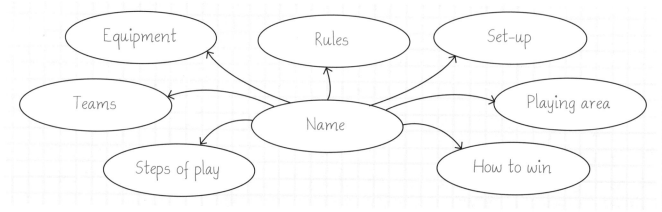

2. Use your mind map to write the first draft of your procedure.

B Debate: 'PE is the least important subject in the Primary School curriculum.'

Make Your Own Wormery

Comprehension Strategies

A Before reading: How to make

Use the strategy of **Predicting**. Predict the steps for making a wormery from the list of equipment below.

- Old newspaper
- A large glass jar or clear plastic bottle with a lid
- Gravel or small stones
- Moist soil
- Light-coloured sand

- A trowel
- Earthworms
- Grass and old leaves
- Scraps of fruit and vegetables and tea leaves

B During reading: Wow word wall

Use the strategy of **Word Attack**. Record your tricky words as you read and make a 'wow word wall' as a class.

C During reading: Stop and think

Use the strategy of **Questioning**. As you read each section, stop to think:

- Did I understand this section?
- Were there any parts that I didn't understand?
- Could I explain this information to someone else?
- Are there any questions that I need to have answered?

Did I understand this section?

D After reading: Fact or fib?

Use the strategy of **Synthesising**. Write three facts and one fib about the text. Then, in pairs, swap your lists and find each other's fib.

1. _____

2. _____

3. _____

4. _____

Comprehension

 STOP! Use your dictionary to find out the meaning of the **bold** words below.

Make Your Own Wormery

Aim: To make a habitat for earthworms.

Equipment:

- Old newspaper
- A large glass jar or clear plastic bottle with a lid
- Gravel or small stones
- **Moist** soil
- Light-coloured sand
- A trowel
- Earthworms
- Grass and old leaves
- **Scraps** of fruit and vegetables and tea leaves

Diagram:

Earthworms

Grass and leaves

Fruit and vegetable scraps and tea leaves

Soil

Sand

Sand

Soil

Soil

Gravel

Trowel

Lid with holes

Method:

1. Cover your work **surface** with old newspaper.
2. Wash and dry the jar (or bottle).
3. Add gravel to the bottom of the jar.
4. Place a deep layer of moist soil, followed by a layer of sand in the jar.
5. Continue layering the soil and sand like this until there is a space of about 5 cm at the top and **ensuring** that the final layer is soil.
6. Use a trowel to gently dig for earthworms in your garden.
7. Carefully place the earthworms in the wormery.
8. Cover the earthworms with the old leaves, grass, scraps of fruit and vegetables and tea leaves.
9. Ask an adult to make some holes in the lid using a sharp knife. Screw the lid on. A lid can also be made by **securing** cloth over the jar with an elastic band.
10. Leave the wormery in a cool dark place, out of **direct** sunlight, for a week or two.
11. Take out your wormery and **observe**.

Top tip!

Worms are **omnivores**, which means they eat all food types. You shouldn't put meat or fish in your wormery though.

Conclusions:

1. The grass and leaves should have been pulled down into the soil.
2. The sand and soil should now be mixed together.

The wormery demonstrates what happens in the garden. Earthworms help to **transport decaying** plant material into the soil. This gets broken down, making the soil **fertile** and **providing** nutrients to help plants to grow.

A In your copy, go investigate.

1. What is the aim of this activity?

2. List the equipment needed for this activity.

3. How much space should you leave at the top of the jar after the last layer of soil? Why should you do this?

4. Why should you dig for the earthworms gently?

5. At what point should you ask an adult for help with this activity? Why?

6. For how long should you leave the wormery?

B In your copy, give your opinion. {?}

1. Why should you cover your work surface?

2. What do you think the fruit and vegetables are added for?

3. Why do you think you should use layers of soil and light-coloured sand?

4. What conditions do you think earthworms prefer? How do you know this?

5. How do earthworms help plants to grow?

6. Would you like to try this activity? Why/Why not?

C Vocabulary

1. Underline the part of each sentence that has been changed from the text.

   (a) Take out your wormery and see what has happened.

   (b) Keep layering the sand and earth like this.

   (c) Leave the wormery in a cold, gloomy place.

   (d) Cover your work space with recycled newspaper.

   (e) Add small stones to the base of the jar.

   (f) Aim: To make a home for earthworms.

   (g) Carefully put the earthworms in the wormery.

2. In your copy, rewrite the sentences above in the order in which they occur in the text and insert the missing synonyms from the text.

D Cloze procedure: 'Amazing Earthworms'. Fill in the blanks.

Earthworms are _____ important part of a garden's ecosystem. They keep the _____ fertilised, which helps plants to grow. They do this by burrowing deep _____ the soil, mixing decaying plant matter from the surface _____ the topsoil and subsoil. _____ prefer damp, cool, dark conditions. They have no lungs and so _____ through their skin. They may live up to eight _____, although one to two is more common. Charles Darwin studied them _____ thirty-nine years and decided that life on _____ would not be possible without their help in fertilising soil and reducing plant waste. Earthworms _____ amazing!

Phonics – 'y' or 'i'

Do you remember all of the different sounds that '**y**' makes? Sometimes we mix up '**y**' and '**i**', because they can make the same sounds.

- '**i**' can make an /**ee**/ sound, usually in the **middle** of a word, e.g. happiness.
- '**y**' can also make an /**ee**/ sound, usually at the **end** of a word, e.g. money.
- '**y**' can make a long /**i**/ sound, usually at the **end** of a word, e.g. my.
- '**y**' can make a short /**i**/ sound, usually in the **middle** of a word e.g. bicycle.

A Use 'y' or 'i' to complete each word.

/ee/		Long /i/		Short /i/	
curl__	aud__ence	dragonfl__	t__ger	gu__tar	s__mbol
cur__osity	mould__	multipl__	__sland	g__m	__guana

B Complete the i/y crossword.

Across

2. A cuboid used to build walls (b)

4. Song sung to help children sleep (l)

5. Physical indication of an illness (s)

8. A scientist's workplace (l)

9. Words to a song (l)

Down

1. Making no noise (s)

3. A mammal carried in its mother's pouch from birth, e.g. a kangaroo (m)

6. To make something appear bigger (m)

7. The inside of something (i)

C In your copy, write a sentence using each of the i/y words above.

Grammar – Conjunctions

A **conjunction** is a word used to join words, phrases or parts of a sentence together. It can help make a sentence more interesting, e.g. I listen to music **while** I walk home.

A conjunction can be used at the beginning of a sentence, with a comma to join the two parts, e.g. **Although** it often tries to bite me, I enjoy playing with my neighbour's cat.

Sometimes conjunctions work together, e.g. I arrived at school **just as** the bell rang.

A Use the conjunctions below to complete the sentences.

whereas	in order to	neither	even though	no sooner than
since	assuming that	unless	nor	what with

1. Julia doesn't like to sing   she is very good at it.
2. I eat   pizza   chips, as they are unhealthy.
3.   I had arrived at the park, it began to rain.
4. I like to play soccer,   my sister enjoys rugby.
5. Amanda, could I have your homework,   it is finished?
6. David sets his alarm five minutes early   be on time for school.
7. Daniel wears a lot of sun cream   he got sunburned last summer.
8. "I would like to borrow this book,   you are reading it," Ruby said.
9. Anna is very fit,   all the exercise she does after school

B In your copy, complete the sentences using the conjunctions below. Write an ending for each sentence that you think is suitable.

by the time	then	while	because	before	until	in case	but

1. I need to go to the hospital   …
2. Elaine always liked to play football   …
3. I would love to come to your birthday party   …
4. The film was long over   …
5. I make sure I bring a spare pair of glasses   …
6. First, Cathal made sure the coast was clear,   …
7. Kelly ran away from the scene of the crime   …

C Dictation: Listen to your teacher and write the sentences in your copy.

 I can do this!
 I'm getting there.
 I need help!

Oral Language

A Missing information

In pairs, describe the steps of something and have your partner guess what you are describing. The winner is the person who can guess correctly with the least number of clues, e.g:

- First, empty the contents of the tin into a saucepan.
- Turn on the ring at a medium heat.
- Meanwhile, put some bread in the toaster.
- Make sure to keep stirring.
- When the toast has popped, butter it.
- Once the _____ are warm, pour them over the toast and enjoy.

Answer: How to make beans on toast

Writing Genre – Procedural Writing

The **language of a procedure** should include:

- nouns and pronouns that refer to general and specific items, e.g. equipment, the earthworms, it.
- the reader referred to in a general way, e.g. you, each player. The reader may not be referred to at all, e.g. dig, hop.
- command action verbs in the present tense, e.g. run, place, find.
- time words, e.g. next, meanwhile, then.
- detailed, factual adjectives, e.g. moist soil, dark cupboard.
- adverbs that describe how, where and when, e.g. quickly, on a soft surface, while it cools.

A Review, edit and rewrite your game instructions.

1. Make sure that your instructions have all of the following:
   - Aim
   - Equipment
   - Method/steps of play
   - Evaluation
   - Procedural language

2. Read over your instructions and edit them for spelling, punctuation and grammar.

3. Rewrite your instructions and include a labelled diagram.

4. Check your work using the procedure self-assessment checklist.

B Play the game.

Ask your teacher if you can teach your new game as part of your PE warm-up. If this isn't possible, maybe you could teach it to your friends in the yard.

The Party Invitation

Comprehension Strategies

A Before reading: I wonder ...

Use the strategy of **Questioning**. Fill in the thought bubbles with questions about the text.

I wonder

I wonder

I wonder

B During reading: This reminds me of ...

Use the strategy of **Making Connections**. While reading, stop along the way to make connections to the characters.

- "This reminds me of a time I ..."
- "This makes me think about when ..."
- "This makes me feel ... because of the time ..."

This makes me think about when ...

C After reading: Crystal ball

Use the strategy of **Predicting**. Look at the title and illustration and use your crystal ball to predict what will happen in the text.

I predict that ...

I imagine that ...

I wonder if ...

I think that ...

I think that ... will happen, because ...

Maybe ... will happen, because ...

D After reading: Developing dialogue

Use the strategy of **Inferring**. In pairs, pick two characters from the text and decide on a dialogue between them. First, decide what has happened since the events shown in the text. Then, use evidence from the text to decide what they will say, how they will react to each other and what will happen as a result of their conversation. Present this to the class and then discuss the differences in dialogue as a class.

Comprehension

The Party Invitation

Sarah: Hey Amal, how r u?

Amal: Hi Sarah I'm so sad, can't believe 2day was our last day!

Sarah: I no!!!! can you believe Miss Murphy cried?? lol

Amal: I thought it was sweet. I'll miss her, she was a gr8 teacher

Sarah: She was ok I guess

Amal: I'm excited for secondary school already ... you're going 2 St Mary's 2 rite?

Sarah: Yeah, it'll be gr8 to have the whole gang there

Amal: Well the whole gang except Lily. I'm so sad her dad's making her go to the all-girls school

Sarah: Oh well. So look, my mam is letting me have a party 2nite. Everyone from our class is coming

Amal: Cool!!! Your mam is the best. I'd never be allowed have a party

Sarah: There'll be food and my dad got a karaoke machine. Should be a gd laugh

Amal: Sounds great!

Sarah: Obviously I'm inviting you

Amal: Yey!!

Sarah: The only thing is, you can't tell Lily

Amal: Oh

Sarah: Yeah, soz! It's just for ppl going to our school nxt yr you c

Lily: Hiya Amal!

Amal: Oh, hi Lily!

Lily: What r u doing tonight?

Amal: Nothing much ...

Lily: Cool, want to hang out? Dad gave me some €€€ to celebrate. He said he'd drop us into the town. We could see a film?

Amal: That's so nice of him!

Lily: I no. He said he's really proud of us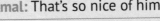

Sarah: Amal??? Can you come r not?

Lily: So, want to come??

A In your copy, go investigate.

1. Whose mobile phone is shown in this story? How do you know this?
2. What is the 'last day' that Amal and Sarah are talking about?
3. How do the girls know Miss Murphy?
4. What secondary school will Sarah and Amal be attending?
5. Why does Sarah say that Lily can't come to her party?
6. Why did Lily's dad give her some money?

B In your copy, give your opinion.

1. Do you think Sarah is a nice person? Explain.
2. How do you think Lily would feel if she knew about the party?
3. How would you feel if you were Amal?
4. What should Amal do?
5. What might happen if she does this?
6. Have you ever been in a situation like this? What did you do?

C Vocabulary

1. Sometimes we use abbreviations (shortened words) while texting. Write the full word for the abbreviations that Sarah, Amal and Lily use in their texts.

   (a) u: _____   **(b)** 2day: _____   **(c)** gr8: _____

   (d) r: _____ and   **(e)** gd: _____   **(f)** soz: _____

2. In what situations do you think you should not use abbreviations in your writing?

   _____

D Cloze procedure: 'The History of Texting'. Fill in the blanks.

Texting, or SMS (short message service), is a form of communication that sends _____ between mobile phones. The maximum length of a text message is 160 characters (_____, numbers or symbols), but modern apps (applications) mean that most people don't have to worry about keeping their messages _____. The first _____ was sent in 1992. As mobile phones at that time didn't have keypads, it was _____ on a computer. It read, '_____ Christmas'. Nokia was the _____ manufacturer to support the sending of SMS messages. In 1997, it _____ the first company to produce a _____ with a full keypad. In 1995, the average American sent only 0.4 texts per month. By 2007, people had begun to send and receive more texts _____ phone calls.

Phonics – Soft 'c'

'c' makes a soft / s / sound when it meets and 'e', 'i', or 'y', e.g. **c**elebrate, pen**c**il, spi**c**y.

'c' makes a hard / k / sound in most other words.

A Tick to show if the 'c' makes a hard sound or a soft sound.

	Hard	Soft		Hard	Soft
1. city			11. curtain		
2. country			12. decide		
3. classroom			13. elegance		
4. advice			14. announcement		
5. cricket			15. cartoon		
6. crocodile			16. candle		
7. percentage			17. cancellation		
8. performance			18. celebrity		
9. compass			19. cardigan		
10. democracy			20. encyclopaedia		

B Complete each word using 's' or 'c'. Check using a dictionary.

entran__e	__uitca__e	fragran__e	a__teroid	violen__e
gro__eries	roman__e	con__equen__e	peri__cope	di__tan__e

C Cross out the incorrect word. Use your dictionary to check the meaning of each word.

1. My piano teacher reminded me to **practise** / **practice** over the weekend.

2. The scientist worked hard to **devise** / **device** a cure for the disease.

3. "I **advise** / **advice** you be careful," called the skiing instructor.

4. Sylvia completes her spellings **practice** / **practise** every night.

5. My mum always gives me great **advice** / **advise**.

6. Rob has a **devise** / **device** that tracks his running time.

Top tip!

'se' usually means that the word is a verb and 'ce' usually means that it is a noun.

Grammar – Sentences

A **clause** is a group of words that make part of, or a whole sentence. A clause must have a verb and a **subject** (the noun or pronoun doing the verb) and usually an **object** (the noun or pronoun that receives the verb). A sentence must make sense by itself.

A **simple sentence** contains one clause, e.g. Rory hates dogs. He likes my pug.

A **compound sentence** contains two simple sentences joined by a **conjunction**, e.g. Rory hates dogs, **though** he likes my pug.

A In your copy, change each simple sentence to a compound sentence by adding a conjunction and another clause.

1. The man is very clumsy _____ ...

2. Megan acted very bravely _____ ...

3. John went for a walk _____ ...

4. The artist is very successful _____ ...

5. My dad weeded our garden _____ ...

6. I visited my cousin _____ ...

A **complex sentence** contains a main clause and a less important clause that would not make sense by itself.

Examples: We played all day, while the sun shone.

Gabriella, upon arriving home, collapsed on the couch.

B Cross out the less important clause from each sentence so that the main clause remains and the sentence still makes sense.

1. My new laptop, which I bought last week, is much better than my old one.

2. As he walked to the bus, Paul remembered he hadn't locked the door.

3. I wish I had studied harder, thought Alison during the test.

4. The lightning bolt that followed the thunder frightened the dog.

5. I finally finished my homework, which was difficult.

6. Even though my sister says it's for kids, my favourite film is 'Cinderella'.

C Complex sentences are more interesting. In your copy, add a less important clause to each sentence to make it a complex sentence.

1. Colm went swimming every day.

2. Isobel broke her leg.

3. I arrived at the airport.

4. I found my favourite shoes.

D Dictation: Listen to your teacher and write the sentences in your copy.

I can do this!   I'm getting there.   I need help!

95

Oral Language

A Giving messages

In pairs, role-play two people giving messages over the phone. Think about the messages these people might be giving and how the nature of the messages or their relationship may affect the way they speak to each other.

1. Mum and Dad
2. Cinderella and her Fairy Godmother
3. Ursula and the Gardaí
4. Fred and his boss

Writing Genre – To Socialise

The purpose of a **text used to socialise** is to maintain or improve relationships or to send a message. A socialising text may be formal or informal.

Structure:

- **Orientation** – The reason for contact; can also include a greeting or time and place.
- **Body** – Contains the main message.
- **Prompt** – Includes instructions about what to do next.

A Plan and write a letter.

1. Choose between the following two options:

   (a) Write a letter to yourself ten years from now.

   (b) Write a letter to your classmates in your new secondary school.

2. Plan your letter under the following headings:

   - Orientation – Reason for contact
   - Body   – Main message you would like to convey, e.g:

     What you hope you have achieved (college, job, travel, etc.)

     Your hobbies, what you are excited about for secondary school, etc.

   - Prompt – Include some questions and how they might respond, e.g:

     What is technology like in the future?

     What are your classmates interested in?

   - Don't forget to include a greeting and a farewell.

3. Write the first draft of your letter using the headings above.

B Drama: Conscience Alley

The class stands in two lines, creating a Conscience Alley. In the role of Amal, a pupil walks through Conscience Alley. One side of the alley will try to convince Amal to go to the party. The other will try to convince her to go to the cinema with Lily. Before taking part in the Conscience Alley, both sides should brainstorm what they will say to Amal to convince her to listen to them.

Oh! The Places You'll Go 17

Comprehension Strategies

A Before reading: Changing images

Use the strategy of **Visualising**. Draw a picture to show what you can picture …

Before reading	During reading	After reading

B During reading: I think … because …

Use the strategy of **Inferring**. While reading, stop along the way to make inferences using evidence from the text.

- "Reading between the lines, I think that … because …"
- "The poet says … but I think he means … because …"
- I think the poet is trying to tell me … because …"

> I think …

C After reading: Main-idea pyramid

Use the strategies of **Determining Importance** and **Summarising**. As a class, brainstorm the main points of the text on post-it notes. Group these points into categories and place them at the bottom of a pyramid. Combine the grouped points into one point on the next level of the pyramid. Keep doing this until one point remains.

D After reading: This makes me feel …

Use the strategies of **Making Connections** and **Visualising**. Read back over the text and try to make connections.

- "This reminds me of …"
- "This makes me think about …"
- "This makes me feel … because …"

On a sheet of paper, draw a picture to show what connections you have made with the text, especially how it makes you feel. Pick one line (or quote) from the text that you connected with especially and write it somewhere in or around your picture. As a class, you could display your pictures at your graduation.

Comprehension

STOP! Use your dictionary to find out the meaning of the **bold** words below.

Oh! The Places You'll Go

Congratulations!

Today is your day.

You're off to Great Places!

You're off and away!

You have brains in your head.

You have feet in your shoes.

You can steer yourself

Any direction you choose.

You're on your own. And you know what you know.

And YOU are the guy who'll decide where to go.

You'll look up and down streets. Look 'em over with care.

About some you will say, "I don't choose to go there."

With your head full of brains and your shoes full of feet,

You're too smart to go down any not-so-good street.

And you may not find any

You'll want to go down.

In that case, of course,

You'll head straight out of town.

It's opener there

In the wide open air.

Out there things can happen

And **frequently** do

To people as brainy

And footsy as you.

And when things start to happen,

Don't worry. Don't stew.

Just go right along.

You'll start happening too.

OH! THE PLACES YOU'LL GO!

You'll be on your way up!

You'll be seeing great sights!

You'll join the high fliers

Who soar to high heights.

You won't lag behind, because you'll have the speed.

You'll pass the whole gang and you'll soon take the **lead**.

Wherever you fly, you'll be the best of the best.

Wherever you go, you will top all the rest.

Except when you don't

Because, sometimes, you won't. [...]

You'll get mixed up, of course,

As you already know.

You'll get mixed up

With many strange birds as you go.

So be sure when you step.

Step with care and great tact

And remember that Life's

A Great Balancing Act.

Just never forget to be dexterous and deft.

And never mix up your right foot with your left.

And will you succeed?

Yes! You will, indeed!

(98 and ¾ percent **guaranteed**.)

KID, YOU'LL MOVE MOUNTAINS!

So ...

Be your name Buxbaum or Bixby or Bray

Or Mordecai Ali Van Allen O'Shea,

You're off to Great Places!

Today is your day!

Your mountain is waiting.

So ... get on your way!

(By Dr Seuss)

A In your copy, go investigate.

1. Who wrote this poem?

2. What can you do if you don't find any streets to go down?

3. What should you do if 'things start to happen'?

4. How should you step?

5. What are the names that the author lists?

6. Does the author believe in you? How do you know?

B In your copy, give your opinion.

1. What do you think the author means by 'You'll get mixed up'?

2. What do you think the author means by 'You'll move mountains'?

3. 'The places you'll go' might be a metaphor. What do you think this might be a metaphor for?

4. What goals do you want to achieve?

5. What might make it difficult for you to achieve your goals?

6. Have you learned anything from this poem? What?

C Vocabulary

1. Highlight all of the rhyming words in the poem. Can you see a pattern?

2. Find a word in the text associated with each of the synonyms and antonyms below.

Word in Text	Synonym	Antonym	Word in Text	Synonym	Antonym
	often	seldom		tall	low
	clever	stupid		broad	narrow
	odd	normal		caution	inattention
	prosper	fail		clever	stupid

D Cloze procedure: 'Dr Seuss'. Fill in the blanks.

Theodor Seuss Geisel was an American writer and illustrator _____ on March 2nd 1904, who was best known for writing popular children's _____. He took on the pen name Dr _____ while studying at Dartmouth College and the University of Oxford. During World _____ II, he worked at the animation department of the US Army, producing several short films, one of _____ won an Academy Award. Seuss wrote many well-_____ children's books such _____ 'Horton Hears a Who!', 'The Cat in the Hat' and 'How the Grinch Stole Christmas'. He published over 60 books _____ his career. His books have _____ over 600 million copies, have been translated into more than 20 _____ and many have been adapted into TV specials and popular films.

Phonics – 'ch'

'ch' can make different sounds: / ch /, e.g. chair, / k /, e.g. school, / sh /, e.g. machine.

Top tip!
When 'sch' come together, 'ch' usually makes a / k / sound.

A Decide whether each 'ch' word makes a /ch/, /k/ or /sh/ sound and write it in the correct list.

chimney	choir	moustache	orchestra	ketchup	parachute
scheme	cheerleader	chalet	hopscotch	brochure	avalanche
slouch	psychic	chandelier	architecture	chef	charisma
chute	headache	sketch	chauffer	itchy	mechanic

/ ch / – chair	/ k / – school	/ sh / – machine

B Use the 'ch' words from the /sh/ sound list above to label these.

_____ _____ _____ _____ _____

C Use some of the 'ch' words in section A to complete these.

1. My friend is really rich. She has a _____ to cook for her, a _____ to drive her around and a huge _____ hanging from her ceiling.

2. Handa wants to study _____ in college. She loves to _____ beautiful buildings in her notebook.

3. The thief came down the _____ , causing an _____ of soot.

4. "Oh no!" cried Michelle. "My car has broken down. I'll call a _____ ."

5. Laurence sings in a _____ and conducts an _____ at the weekend.

6. I wouldn't like to have a _____ , because it would be _____ on my face.

Grammar – Parts of Speech

An **article** is a word used to refer to a specific or a general noun.

'**The**' is a **definite article**. It describes a specific noun, e.g. Pass **the** milk, please.

'**A**' and '**an**' are **indefinite articles**. They describe a general noun, e.g. Ed has **a** dog.

A Insert the correct definite or indefinite articles in these sentences. Ring the definite articles and underline the indefinite articles.

1. Bill and Ted have gone to   park to play   GAA match.

2. Could I borrow   pencil? I lost   one I bought yesterday.

3. "I have   idea!" called Margaret. "We should go to   zoo."

4. I haven't been to   cinema in ages. I would love to go and see   film.

5. We should leave soon, because it takes   hour to get to   airport.

An **interjection** is a word that shows emotion or feeling. It is often followed by an exclamation mark, e.g. Agh! Oh no! Oops! Whoa! Hmm!

B Use an interjection and the correct punctuation to complete these.

1.   said Kasper when he dropped his glasses.

2.   I've lost my favourite necklace!" moaned Mrs Deegan.

3.   exclaimed Orla, as she looked at the fireworks display.

4.   I'm not sure I believe your story," said the boys' teacher.

5.   cried Angela when her brother jumped out and scared her.

There are nine main **parts of speech**: "Hello!" (interjection) **said** (verb) **Dermot** (noun) happily (adverb) **when** (conjunction) **he** (pronoun) **met** (verb) @ (article) **boy** (noun) **from** (preposition) **his** (adjective) **class** (noun).

C Colour the words to show the parts of speech using the colours above. Look back over the grammar pages of this book to help you.

1. "Okay, boys and girls, sit down quickly," called Mr Higgins sternly.

2. "This is an important test, because secondary schools always look at it," he announced.

3. "Oh no!" Thought Claudia desperately. "I forgot about the test!"

D Dictation: Listen to your teacher and write the sentences in your copy.

 I can do this!   I'm getting there.   I need help!

101

Oral Language

A Graduation invitations

Think of a guest you would like to invite to your 6th Class graduation. This person could be famous, living or dead or even fictional. Think of why you would like to invite them and why they should come. Create a real invitation including all of this information. Decorate it and include all of the parts of a text used to socialise. As a class, present your invitations and have your teacher or another class pick the winner. They can judge it based on the presentations, the design, the reasons for inviting each guest and how convincing the invitation might be to this guest.

Writing Genre – To Socialise

The **language of a text used to socialise** should include:
- first- and second-person pronouns, e.g. I, you, we.
- a specific subject, e.g. Sarah, Mr Lynch.
- questions or statements of inquiry, e.g. How are you? I hope you are well.
- brief, simple language.
- simple past tense (future tense should be used in invitations).
- action verbs, e.g. visited, arranged.
- words to show time, e.g. then, next week.
- a formal or an informal tone, depending on the audience, e.g. See you soon, Yours sincerely.
- It may also include personal endearments or statements of sentiment, e.g. dear, we miss you, as well as abbreviations or pictograms (emojis), e.g. c u l8r, ☺

A Review, edit and rewrite your letter to your future self or your new classmates.

1. Make sure that your letter has all of the following:
   - Orientation ▪ Body ▪ Prompt ▪ A greeting and a farewell ▪ Language used to socialise

2. Read over your letter and edit it for spelling, punctuation and grammar.

3. Rewrite your letter and include your current address and your future address or the address of your new school.

4. Check your work using the 'to socialise' self-assessment checklist.

B Art activity

Taking the poem 'Oh! The Places You'll Go' as your inspiration, create an artwork of you in a hot air balloon travelling to all of the places you want to go and showing the goals that you hope to achieve. You could make the balloon using papier-mâché and hang it in front of a map that you have painted. Take a photograph or draw a picture of yourself and place it in a paper basket hanging from the balloon.

Revision and Assessment

Revision: Grammar and Phonics

Look back at the grammar on pages 53, 59, 65, 71, 77, 83, 89, 95 and 101.

Day 1

1. Ring the words that need a capital letter and add the missing punctuation.

   (a) where have you been   alex asked dad

   (b) ha ha that film was hilarious

2. Tick for the underlined word.

   (a) I ate popcorn <u>during</u> the film.

   Preposition   Pronoun

   (b) That is <u>ours</u>.

   Adjective   Pronoun

   (c) The <u>feeble</u> old man hobbled away.

   Adjective   Preposition

3. Order the adjectives correctly.

   (a) woollen, ugly, old

   The _____, _____, _____ hat

   (b) little, beautiful, furry

   The _____, _____, _____ dog

4. Ring the correct spelling.

   (a) sequential / sequencial

   (b) glacial / glatial

5. Match the rhyming words.

(a) pie ▪	▪ blend
(b) friend ▪	▪ creature
(c) teacher ▪	▪ buy

6. Change to verbs with '-ate'.

   (a) assassin: _____

   (b) nomination: _____

   (c) formula: _____

   (d) participant: _____

Day 2

1. Ring the words that need a capital letter and add the missing punctuation.

   (a) a chicken cheese and ham sandwich please

   (b) ouch said sam you stood on my toe

2. Tick for the underlined word/s.

   (a) You may go, <u>assuming that</u> you are done.

   Adverb   Conjunction

   (b) I'm <u>almost</u> finished my dinner.

   Adverb   Conjunction

3. Preposition of where or when?

   (a) throughout   Where   When

   (b) after   Where   When

   (c) beneath   Where   When

4. Tick the correct type of sentence.

   (a) As she walked home, Kim tripped.

   Simple   Complex

   (b) Carlos likes to fish.

   Simple   Compound

   (c) I went to the park and saw my friend.

   Compound   Complex

5. Write the heteronym.

   (a) to argue

   to move a boat with oars _____

   (b) produced when crying

   to rip paper or material _____

103

Revision: Grammar and Phonics

Day 3

1. Insert the correct relative pronoun: whose or that.

   (a) The man _____ wallet was stolen

   (b) The cat _____ caught the mouse

2. Insert the correct article: a, an or the.

   (a) I can play _____ guitar.

   (b) Georgina has _____ pet goldfish.

   (c) I rode in _____ ambulance.

3. Complete each simile.

   (a) As white as a _____

   (b) Fits like a _____

   (c) Clean as a _____

4. Change to nouns with '-ance' or '-ence'.

   (a) relevant: _____

   (b) evident: _____

   (c) fragrant: _____

   (d) eloquent: _____

5. Match the correct 'y' sound: syrup, pharmacy, qualify, yawn.

   (a) **ee**: _____

   (b) Long **i**: _____

   (c) Short **i**: _____

   (d) **yuh**: _____

6. Hard or soft 'c'?

   (a) classroom   Hard   Soft

   (b) city   Hard   Soft

   (c) advice   Hard   Soft

   (d) cricket   Hard   Soft

7. Ring the correct spelling.

   (a) audience / audyence

   (b) simbol / symbol

Day 4

1. Match the adjectives to the correct type: away, joyfully, completely, tomorrow, always.

   (a) Manner: _____

   (b) Place: _____

   (c) Time: _____

   (d) Degree: _____

   (e) Frequency: _____

2. Insert the interjection and add punctuation: Hey, Ouch, Oh no.

   (a) _____ I can't find my homework.

   (b) _____ Give that back.

   (c) _____ I got a paper cut.

3. Tick the correct conjunction.

   (a) I have red hair _____ my sister is blonde.

   in case   whereas   what with

   (b) _____ I had stepped outside, it started to rain.

   no sooner than   unless   since

   (c) I train hard _____ make the school team.

   so   assuming that   in order to

4. Match the correct /ch/ sound: scheme, slouch, parachute.

   (a) **ch**: _____

   (b) **sh**: _____

   (c) **k**: _____

5. Change to adjectives with '-cial' or '-tial'.

   (a) essence: _____

   (b) torrent: _____

   (c) benefit: _____

Assessment: Phonics

A **Ring the correct spelling.**

1. I received a **fracture** / **fracsure** to my wrist when I crashed my bike.

2. The **orchestra** / **orkestra** performed wonderfully last night.

3. Connor's cricket coach thinks that he shows great **potencial** / **potential**.

4. Emojis are **symbols** / **simbols** used to make texts more interesting.

5. I used a **broshure** / **brochure** to plan my holiday to Disneyland.

6. The **dragonfly** / **dragonfli** is a beautiful insect.

7. There are a lot of **artificial** / **artifitial** flavourings in ready meals.

8. There is a beautiful **fragranse** / **fragrance** from those flowers.

9. The gorillas in Dublin Zoo have a really big **enclosure** / **encloture**.

10. '**Curiosity** / **Curiocity** killed the cat' is a phrase that means 'don't be nosy'.

`10`

B **Write the correct heteronym.**

1. The current moment
   To give a gift

   1. _____

2. A white pigeon-like bird
   Past tense of 'dive'

   2. _____

3. A hair decoration
   Bending the body to show respect

   3. _____

4. Extremely small
   One-sixtieth of an hour

   4. _____

`4`

C **Add '-ate', '-cial' or '-tial' to each root word.**

'-ate' verb		'-cial' or '-tial' adjective			
origin		species		resident	
complication		society		office	
refrigerator		influence		sequence	

`9`

D **Match the rhyming words.**

1. boar ▪	▪ cold	5. leaf ▪	▪ square
2. flower ▪	▪ photo	6. hair ▪	▪ rule
3. mould ▪	▪ floor	7. tissue ▪	▪ chew
4. blow ▪	▪ our	8. school ▪	▪ thief

`8`

Assessment: Comprehension

Perseus and Medusa – A Greek Myth

Many years ago in Greece, there lived a young man named Perseus. The old king, Polydectes, wanted to marry Perseus's beautiful mother, Danae, against her will and would only agree to release her if Perseus brought him the head of Medusa. Medusa was a gorgon, a terrifying monster with the body and face of a beautiful woman, but with hundreds of snakes for hair and the power to turn anyone who looked her in the eye to stone. Brave Perseus accepted this challenge, thinking only of his mother's happiness.

No sooner had Perseus set out on his journey than he met Hermes, the Messenger God, and Athena, the Goddess of War and Wisdom. Hermes handed Perseus a host of useful gifts.

"These winged sandals will carry you to Medusa's cave. Wear this helmet for invisibility when you get there and use this sack to carry her severed head," said Hermes.

Perseus thanked Hermes and turned to Athena. "You will need these also," she said, handing him a sword and a bronze shield so well polished that he could see his own reflection in it.

Perseus strapped on the sandals and marvelled as they carried him to the mouth of Medusa's cave. When he landed, he pulled the helmet down firmly onto his head, instantly becoming invisible. Not wanting to be turned to stone like those who had come before him, Perseus used the reflection in the shield to find his way. Feeling scared, but ready to face the gorgon, he made his way cautiously into the cave.

Before long, Perseus came upon Medusa. She heard his footsteps on the cave floor and whirled around to face him, but could not see him. Perseus lunged at her, but could not find his aim while watching her reflection in the shield. He managed only to remove a few hissing snake heads. As Medusa roared with frustration, Perseus kicked a stone towards the back of the cave. Medusa's head whipped around at the noise behind her. Perseus took his chance and darted forward. This time his aim was true. His sword sliced easily through her neck and her fearsome head fell to the floor with a thud.

Careful not to look her in the eye even in death, Perseus bundled the head into the sack that Hermes had given him and set off home to free his mother.

"Impossible!" cried the king, upon Perseus's return. "There is no way a weakling like you could have beaten a monster such as Medusa."

"See for yourself," cried Perseus, pulling Medusa's head from the sack and turning the king and all of his subjects to stone where they sat.

Assessment: Comprehension and Vocabulary

A In your copy, go investigate.

1. Did Perseus want the king to marry his mother? How do you know?
2. In your opinion, which was the most useful item that Perseus received? Explain.
3. What made it difficult for Perseus to battle Medusa?
4. Do you think Perseus was clever? Explain with evidence from the text.
5. Did the king expect Perseus to return? What makes you think this?
6. How would you describe Perseus? Use examples from the story.

6

B Vocabulary: Ring the correct synonym.

1. hesitated:	paused	squandered	hastened	quenched
2. cautious:	tentative	gallant	reckless	busy
3. typical:	winding	dazzling	abnormal	commonplace
4. harmful:	simple	beneficial	timid	detrimental
5. permitted:	prohibited	replied	approved	reliable
6. direct:	sturdy	expensive	ambiguous	straightforward
7. frequently:	clever	seldom	often	cautious
8. abash:	soothe	saunter	upset	embarrass

8

C Cloze procedure: 'A Trip to the Circus'. Fill in the blanks.

It was the start of the summer _____ and Jan and Belma were going to the circus to celebrate finishing 6th _____. They paid four euro each for their _____ and bought come candy floss with their _____. They took their seats on the long benches and waved to _____ of the other kids from their class, who were sitting across _____ them. At last, the lights went down and the show began. "Ugh, I hate _____. They creep me out," said Jan as _____ clowns juggled _____ in front of them. Next came the acrobats. They wowed the crowd by swinging upside down by their _____. Finally, the ringmaster's son was introduced. He performed amazing tricks, flips and tumbles on a _____. Suddenly, something went wrong. He landed awkwardly from of a high jump and _____ off to the side, out of control. The crowd gasped and then cheered as he _____ one of the acrobat's swings to save himself. He flipped to the ground, _____ deeply as the crowd _____.

15

Assessment: Grammar

A **In each of the sentences below:**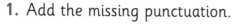

Punctuation

8

1. Add the missing punctuation.

2. Find an adjective, a pronoun, a preposition and an adverb or a conjunction

  (a) You all gave a beautiful performance   announced the director excitedly

  (b) I checked underneath the bed   even though I didn't leave it there

  (c) Lucy always shares her meagre lunch with whomever needs it

  (d) The man jumped between the pillars just as the cars roared past

Adjective	Pronoun	Preposition	Adverb	Conjunction

4

B **Ring the mistake/s in each sentence.**

1. The boy whose stole the bike ran away.

2. "Did you see a earthworm," asked a science teacher.

3. The family visited an zoo for Hilarys birthday.

4. Did Jessie Naji and Daniel do her homework!

5. "Hey"! shouted Cara "come back here with my watch"

6. I bought a silk new dress for my mum, because it was his birthday.

15

C **For each of the sentences below:**

1. Tick simple, compound or complex.

2. Ring the subject and underline the object.

  (a) The man listened to music as he walked home.

  (b) While I find it difficult, I enjoy writing poems.

  (c) Andrea bakes cookies every Sunday.

Simple	Compound	Complex

9

D **Complete each simile or metaphor and tick.**

1. I slept like a _____.

2. Don't judge a book by its _____.

3. As cool as a _____.

4. Time _____ when you're having fun.

Simile	Metaphor

4

E **Dictation: Listen to your teacher and write the sentences in your copy.**

 I can do this!   I'm getting there.   I need help!

Dictation

Red indicates phonics covered in the unit.

Green indicates grammar.

Purple indicates an additional activity or a question revising grammar taught recently.

Unit 1: Punctuation and silent letters

1. "Do I have pneumonia?" asked Patricia calmly.

2. During World War Two (II), Hitler designed a campaign to persecute the Jewish people.

3. "I cannot pay the debt I owe to the government, the plumber or the psychiatrist because of this receipt!" cried Mrs Kelly.

Underline the silent letters in these sentences.

Unit 2: Nouns and '-nge'

1. I cringed with embarrassment when my brother started to whinge in the shop.

2. The pride of lions showed grace and elegance as they lunged at their prey in a terrifying exchange.

3. "Arrange the batch of cookies on this plate and bring them into the lounge!" ordered the old woman.

Underline the concrete nouns, ring the abstract nouns and box the collective nouns.

Unit 3: Verbs 1 and homophones

1. Marina swung the bat at the ball so hard that it flew through the air, making a big hole in the wall.

2. I helped with the Junior Infants yesterday by tying their laces and giving them praise for playing nicely.

3. It's good to wear a hat when the weather is hot so that your bare skin doesn't get sunburned.

Ring the present participle and underline the past participle.

Can you think of a homophone for any of the words in these sentences?

Unit 4: Verbs 2, and '-ance' and '-ence'

1. We cycled in silence until we saw the end of the track in the distance.

2. A man will be parking cars at the entrance to the restaurant for the convenience of the people eating there.

3. I have cleaned my room so that I can buy tickets with my allowance and be in the audience when my favourite band performs.

Underline the verbs and name the tense in each sentence.

Find at least one noun in each sentence.

Unit 5: Commas, and '–ancy' and '-ency'

1. Occup**ancy**, resid**ency** and ten**ancy** are all words referring to where you live.

2. "This is a matter of urg**ency**, Mrs Amir," said the principal calmly. "I am calling to discuss your son's tru**ancy** today."

3. **Although** there is rarely an emerg**ency**, Molly has a tend**ency** to call the Gardaí when she hears loud noises.

Underline the concrete nouns and ring the abstract nouns in these sentences.

Unit 6: Singular and plural, and 'multi-', 'mono-', 'multi-' and 'micro-'

1. The **micro**biologist keeps her **micro**scope**s** in **boxes** on the **multi**purpose **shelves**.

2. "I have decided to retire from making **movies**," announced the **mega**star in a **mono**tone voice.

3. "I would like to buy these **multi**coloured **houses**," said Rory as he played **Mono**poly with his **children**.

Ring the plural nouns in these sentences and change them to singular.

Unit 7: Apostrophes, and '-ary', '-ery' and '-ory'

1. The two girl**s**' access**ory** boxes were stolen during the robb**ery**.

2. Jame**s's** parents are celebrating their fourteenth wedding anniver**sary**. The traditional gift for this is iv**ory**.

3. I could**'ve** gone to the party in the second**ary** school to celebrate their team**'s** vict**ory** if I had**n't** had surg**ery**.

Ring the plural nouns in these sentences and change them to singular.

Unit 8: Assessment

1. A huge audience will be attending the heroes' party to celebrate their bravery on Sunday. (Note: Pupils may need to be told that there is more than one hero.)

2. "Studying accountancy in Dublin isn't my preference for college," said Mia to her principal with conviction.

3. Our school knew how much they had paid for the megaphones, microphones and dictionaries, because they had received a receipt.

Make a list of nouns and verbs in these sentences.

State the tense of each sentence.

Unit 9: Adjectives, and '-sure' and '-ture'

1. Kim was **astounded** when she saw a pic**ture** of **ancient** **buried** trea**sure** in the newspaper.

2. The **slimy**, **putrid**, **green** mix**ture** exploded in the lab, because the scientist didn't mea**sure** it correctly.

3. "It is **cruel** and **immature** to draw an **ugly** carica**ture** of your classmates, Dave," said his teacher disappointedly.

Underline the adjectives in these sentences and write a synonym for each.